COUNTERINSURGENCY
IN ADEN

OTHER BOOKS IN THIS SERIES

Available now at newsagents and booksellers

SOLDIER A SAS: Behind Iraqi
Lines   £4.99 net

SOLDIER B SAS: Heroes of the
South Atlantic   £4.99 net

SOLDIER C SAS: Secret War
in Arabia   £4.99 net

SOLDIER D SAS: The Colombian
Cocaine War   £4.99 net

SOLDIER E SAS: Sniper Fire
in Belfast   £4.99 net

SOLDIER F SAS: Guerrillas in
the Jungle   £4.99 net

SOLDIER G SAS: The Desert
Raiders   £4.99 net

SOLDIER H SAS: The Headhunters
of Borneo   £4.99 net

SOLDIER I SAS: Eighteen Years in
the Elite Force   £4.99 net

SOLDIER J: SAS

COUNTERINSURGENCY IN ADEN

Shaun Clarke

First published in Great Britain 1994
22 Books, 3 Sheldon Way, Larkfield, Maidstone, Kent

Copyright © 1994 by 22 Books

A CIP catalogue record for this book is available from the
British Library

ISBN 1 898125 13 9

10 9 8 7 6 5 4 3 2 1

Typeset by Hewer Text Composition Services, Edinburgh
Printed and bound in Great Britain by
Caledonian International Book Manufacturing Ltd, Glasgow

Prelude

The port of Aden is located on a peninsula enclosing the eastern side of Bandar at-Tawahi, Aden's harbour. It is bounded to the west and north-west by Yemen, to the north by the great desert known as the Rub' al-Khali, the Empty Quarter, to the east by Oman, and to the south by the Gulf of Aden and the Arabian Sea. Though a centre of trade since the days of antiquity, and mentioned in the Bible, the city in 1964 looked less than appealing.

Standing beside his wife, Miriam, on the deck of the P & O liner *Himalaya*, Norman Blakely, emigrating to Australia from Winchester, where he had taught ancient history at the renowned public school, realized he had known all these facts since his own school days. He certainly recognized the features he had often read about, yet he felt a

1

certain disappointment at what he was seeing, not least the surprising modernity of the place.

Even from this distance, beyond the many rowing boats and motor launches dotted about the mud-coloured waters of the harbour, Aden was no more than an untidy sprawl of white-painted stone tower buildings and warehouses surrounded by an ugly clutter of jibs and cranes, immense oil tanks and huge lights raised high on steel gantries – all hemmed in on two sides by the promontories of Jebel Shamsan (Aden) and Jebel Ihsan (Little Aden). Both of these short necks of bleached volcanic rock thrust out from, and were dominated by, an equally unattractive maritime mountain range that varied from 1000 to 2000 feet and was constantly shadowed by depressing grey clouds.

Rising up the lower slopes of the mountains behind the town, about a mile beyond it, was a roughly triangular maze of low, white-painted buildings, which Norman assumed was the old commercial centre known as the Crater. What he did not know – even though he and the other passengers had received a leaflet gently warning them of the 'occasional' dangers of Aden – is that it was the home of the most dangerous anti-British terrorists in that troublesome country.

'If the town's as depressing as it looks from here,' Norman said to Miriam, 'we'll take a taxi up to the Crater. It's almost certainly less commercialized than Aden proper – and hopefully more like the real thing.'

'That leaflet said not to wander too far from the port area,' Miriam reminded him.

'The authorities *always* exaggerate these situations for their own reasons,' Norman said with conviction. 'In this instance, they doubtless want us to remain in the port area because that's where all the duty-free goods are sold. They just want to make money. Such goods aren't sold up in the Crater, so that's where we'll go.'

Trade in a particular kind of duty-free goods was already taking place in the water below them, where the 'bum boats' were packed tightly together by the hull of their ship and stacked high with a colourful collection of souvenirs and other cheap merchandise piled high in wooden crates and cardboard boxes. On offer were 'hand-tooled' – in fact, mass-produced – leather purses and wallets; cartons of Senior Service, Players, Woodbine and Camel cigarettes; Zenith 8 x 30 binoculars, sold in sealed boxes, many of which were fake and did not work; 35mm SLR cameras; transistor radios; counterfeit Rolex wristwatches; and even cartons of Colgate toothpaste. The goods were being sold by shrieking, gesticulating Arabs dressed in a colourful variety of garments, from English shirts and trousers to sarongs and turbans, though all wore thongs about their legs.

The Arabs were bartering by shouting preliminary prices and sending their wares up for inspection in baskets tied to ropes that had been hurled up to the passengers, who had obligingly tied them to the ship's railing. The individual passenger then either lowered the goods back down in the basket or removed them and deposited the agreed amount of money in their place.

While this noisy, good-natured barter was being conducted between the passengers and the Arab vendors below, other passengers were throwing coins into the water between the bum boats and watching Arab children dive from the jetty for them.

Ignoring these activities, Norman led his wife down the swaying gangplank to embark on the sixty-man transit boat that would take them the short distance to the quay. The latter was guarded by uniformed British soldiers, some in shorts, others in lightweight trousers, some armed with

Sten guns or self-loading rifles, others with pistols holstered at their hips.

The sight of the soldiers made Miriam more nervous.

'Are you sure this is wise?' she asked Norman.

'Of course,' he said resolutely, but with a hint of irritation, for his wife was the anxious type. 'Can't let a few tin soldiers bother us. Besides, they're here for our protection, so you've no need to fear.'

'There's a war going on here, dear.'

'Between Yemeni guerrillas and the British army, mostly up in the mountains. Not down *here*, Miriam.' He tugged impatiently at her hand. 'Come on! Let's explore.'

Walking through the arched entrance of the Aden Port Trust, which was guarded by more British troops, Norman and Mariam stepped into Tawahi Main Road, where they were suddenly assailed by the noise of traffic and a disorientating array of signs in Arabic and English. Stuck on the wall by the entrance was a small blue rubbish bin with a notice saying, in English only: Keep Your Town Clean. Another sign said: Aden Field Force – Forging an Empire. Left of the entrance, lined up against a wire-mesh fence surmounted by three strands of menacing barbed wire which protected the building, was a taxi rank whose drivers, all Arabs wearing a mixture of sarongs, turbans and loose shirts, were soliciting custom from the *Himalaya*'s emerging passengers. Other Muslims were carrying with one hand trays piled high with bananas, selling steaming rice-based dishes from blue-painted, wheeled barrows, or dispensing water for a price, dishing it out by the ladleful from a well-scrubbed steel bucket.

An enthusiastic armchair traveller on his first real trip away from home, Norman was keen to see the harbour area, which he knew was called Ma'alah. Politely rejecting the services of the beaming, gesturing taxi drivers, he led his wife through the teeming streets. He was instantly struck by the exotic variety of the people – mostly Sunni Muslims, but with a smattering of Saydi Muslims from the northern tribes of northern Yemen, as well as small groups of Europeans, Hindus and Yemeni Jews.

However, the history teacher was slightly put off by the sheer intensity of the noisy throng, with its cripples, blind men, thieves with amputated hands, grimy, shrieking children, armed soldiers, both British and Federation of South Arabia, along with goats, cows and mangy dogs. He was also disillusioned by the forest of English shop signs above the many stores stacked with duty-free goods. Everywhere they looked, Norman and his increasingly agitated wife saw signs advertising Tissot and Rolex wristwatches, Agfa and Kodak film, BP petrol.

A soldier from the Queen's Own Highlanders, complete with self-loading rifle (SLR), water bottle and grim, watchful face, stood guard at a street corner by the Aden Store Annexe – the sole agent for Venus watches, proudly displayed in their hundreds in the shop window – under a sign showing the latest 35mm cameras. In another street, the London Store, Geneva Store and New Era Store stood side by side – all flat-fronted concrete buildings with slatted curtains over window-shaped openings devoid of glass – with buckets, ladders and the vendors' chairs outside and the mandatory soldiers parading up and down. In a third street, the locals were practically jammed elbow to elbow under antique clocks and signs advertising hi-fi systems, televisions and photographic equipment, while the tourists, either seated on chairs or pressed back against the walls by the tide of passers-by, bartered for tax-free goods, oblivious to the armed troops standing watchfully beside them.

As well as blind and crippled beggars, including one who hopped along on his hands and knees like a human spider, the streets were packed with fast-talking Arabs selling phoney Rolex wristwatches and Parker pens. Honking Mercedes, Jaguars and more modest Volkswagen Beetles all had to make their slow progress not only through the teeming mass of humans, but also through the sea of livestock and undernourished dogs.

Towering over the town, the mountains appeared to run right down to the streets, sun-bleached and purplish in the grey light, with water conduits snaking along their rocky slopes.

Stopping by the Miramar Bazaar, Norman wiped sweat from his face, suddenly realized that the heat was appalling, and decided that he had had enough of this place. Apart from its few remaining Oriental features, it was all much too modern and commercialized for his liking.

'Let's take a taxi to the Crater,' he said.

'It's called Crater,' Miriam corrected him pedantically. 'Not *the* Crater . . . And I don't think we should go up there, dear. It's supposed to be dangerous.'

'Oh, tosh!' Norman said impatiently, eager to see the *real* Aden. 'It can't be any worse than this

8

filthy hole. Besides, you only live once, my love, so let's take our chances.'

So packed was the street with shops, stalls, animals and, above all, people, that the cars could only inch forward, their frustrated drivers hooting relentlessly. It took Norman some time to find a vacant taxi, but eventually the couple were driven out of town, along the foot of the mountains, to arrive a few minutes later at the foetid rabbit warren of Crater.

Merely glancing out the window at the thronging mass of Arabs in the rubbish-strewn street, wreathed in smoke from the many open fires and pungent food stalls, was enough to put Miriam off. She was disconcerted even more to realize, unlike in the harbour area, there were no British soldiers guarding the streets.

'Let's go back, dear,' she suggested, touching Norman's arm.

'Rubbish! We'll get out and investigate,' he insisted.

After the customary haggling, Norman paid the driver and started out of the taxi. However, just as he placed his right foot on the ground, a dark-skinned man wearing an Arab robe, or *futah*, and on his head a *shemagh*, rushed past him, reaching out with his left hand to roughly push him back into the cab.

Outraged, Norman straightened up and was about to step out again when the same Arab reached under his *futah* and took out a pistol with a quick, smooth sweep of his right hand. Spreading his legs to steady himself, he took aim at another Arab emerging from the mud-brick house straight ahead. He fired six shots in rapid succession, punching the victim backwards, almost lifting him off the ground and finally bowling him into the dirt.

Even as Miriam screamed in terror and others bawled warnings or shouted out in fear, the assassin turned back to the deeply shocked couple.

'Sorry about that,' he said in perfect English, then again pushed Norman back into the taxi and slammed the door in his face. He was disappearing back into the crowd as the driver noisily ground his gears, made a sharp U-turn and roared off the way he had come, the dust churned up by his spinning wheels settling over the dead Arab on the ground.

Shocked beyond words, no longer in love with travelling, Norman trembled in the taxi beside his sobbing wife and kept his head down. Mercifully, the taxi soon screeched to a halt at the archway leading into the Aden Port Trust, where their ship was docked.

'He was English!' Norman eventually babbled. 'That Arab was *English*!'

Miriam sobbing hysterically in his arms, he hurried up the gangplank, glad to be back aboard the ship and on his way to Australia.

'He was English!' he whispered, as they were swallowed up by the welcoming vastness of the *Himalaya*.

1

The Hercules C-130 transport plane bounced heavily onto the runway of Khormaksar, the RAF base in Aden. Roaring even louder than ever, with its flaps down, it threw the men in the cramped hold together as it trundled shakily along the runway. Having been flown all the way from their base at Bradbury Lines, Hereford, via RAF Lyneham, Wiltshire, the men of D Squadron SAS were glad to have finally arrived. Nevertheless they cursed a good deal as they sorted out their weapons, water bottles, bergen rucksacks, ammunition belts and other kit, which had been thrown together and become entangled during the rough landing.

'This pilot couldn't ride a bike,' Corporal Ken Brooke complained, 'let alone fly an aeroplane.'

'They're pilots because they're too thick to do anything else,' Lance-Corporal Les Moody replied.

'Stop moaning and get ready to disembark,' Sergeant Jimmy 'Jimbo' Ashman told them. 'That RAF Loadmaster's already preparing to open the door, so we'll be on the ground in a minute or two and you can all breathe fresh air again.'

'Hallelujah!' Ken exclaimed softly.

In charge of the squadron was the relatively inexperienced, twenty-four-year-old Captain Robert Ellsworth. A recent recruit from the Somerset and Cornwall Light Infantry, the young officer had a healthy respect for the superior experience of the troops who had already served the Regiment well in Malaya and Borneo, particularly his two sergeants, Jimmy Ashman and Richard Parker. The former was an old hand who had started as a youngster with the Regiment when it was first formed in North Africa way back in 1941 under the legendary David Stirling. Jimbo was a tough, fair, generally good-natured NCO who understood his men and knew how to get things done.

Parker, known as Dead-eye Dick, or simply Dead-eye, because of his outstanding marksmanship, was more of a loner, forged like steel in the hell of the Telok Anson swamp in Malaya and, more recently, in what had been an equally nightmarish campaign in Borneo. Apart from being the best shot and probably the most feared and admired soldier in the Regiment, Parker was also valuable in that he had spent his time since Borneo at the Hereford and Army School of Languages, adding a good command of Arabic to his other skills.

Another Borneo hand, Trooper Terry Malkin, who had gone there as a 'virgin' but received a Mention in Dispatches for his bravery, was in Aden already, working under cover with one of the renowned 'Keeni-Meeni' squads. As a superior signaller Terry would be sorely missed for the first few weeks, though luckily he would be returning to the squadron in a few weeks' time, when his three-month stint in Aden was over.

Three NCOs who had also been 'broken in' in Borneo, though not with the men already mentioned, were among those preparing to disembark from the Hercules: the impetuous Corporal Ken Brooke, the aptly named Lance-Corporal Les Moody and the medical specialist, Lance-Corporal Laurence 'Larry' Johnson. All were good, experienced soldiers.

Two recently badged troopers, Ben Riley and Dennis 'Taff' Thomas, had been included to make up the required numbers and be trained under the more experienced men. All in all, Captain

Ellsworth felt that he was in good company and hoped to prove himself worthy of them when the campaign began.

The moment the Hercules came to a halt, the doors were pushed open and sunlight poured into the gloomy hold. Standing up with a noisy rattling of weapons, the men fell instinctively into two lines and inched forward, past the stacked, strapped-down supply crates, to march in pairs down the ramp to the ground. Once out of the aircraft, they were forced to blink against the fierce sunlight before they could look about them to see, parked neatly along the runway, RAF Hawker Hunter ground-support aircraft, Shackleton bombers, Twin Pioneer transports, and various helicopters, including the Sikorski S-55 Whirlwind, which the squadron had used extensively in Malaya and Borneo, and the ever-reliable Wessex S-58 Mark 1. Bedford three-ton lorries, Saladin armoured cars and jeeps with rear-mounted Bren light machineguns were either parked near the runway or cruising along the tarmac roads between the corrugated tin hangars and concrete buildings. Beyond the latter could be seen the sun-scorched, volcanic rock mountains that encircled and dominated the distant port of Aden.

The fresh air the men had hoped to breathe after hours in the Hercules was in fact filled with dust. Their throats dried out within seconds, making them choke on the dust when they tried to breathe, and they all broke out in sweat the instant they stepped into the suffocating heat.

'Jesus!' Ken hissed. 'This is worse than Borneo.'

'I feel like I'm burning up,' Les groaned. 'Paying for my sins.'

'Pay for those and you'll burn for ever,' Jimbo told him, breaking away from a conversation with Captain Ellsworth and Sergeant Parker. 'Now pick up your gear and head for those Bedfords lined up on the edge of the runway. We've a long way to go yet.'

'What?' the newly fledged trooper Ben Riley asked in shock, practically croaking in the dreadful humidity and wiping sweat from his face.

'We've a long way to go yet,' Jimbo repeated patiently. 'Sixty miles to our forward base at Thumier, to be exact. And we're going in those Bedfords parked over there.'

'Sixty miles?' Ben asked, as if he hadn't heard the sergeant correctly. 'You mean *now*?'

'That's right, Trooper. Now.'

'Without a break?'

'Naturally, Trooper.'

'I think what he means, Sergeant,' the other recently badged trooper, Taff Thomas, put in timidly, aware that the temperature here could sometimes rise to 150 degrees Fahrenheit, 'is that a two-week period is normally allowed for acclimatization to this kind of heat.'

Ken and Larry laughed simultaneously.

'That's for the bleedin' greens,' Les explained, referring to the green-uniformed regular Army. 'Not for the SAS. We don't expect two weeks' paid leave. We just get up and go.'

'Happy, Troopers?' Jimbo asked. Both men nodded, keen to do the right thing. 'Right, then, get up in those Bedfords.'

The men did as they were told and soon four three-tonners were leaving the RAF base. They were guarded front and rear by British Army 6×6-drive Saladin armoured cars, each with a 76mm QF (quick-firing) gun and a Browning .30-inch machine-gun. The convoy trundled along a road that was lined with coconut palms and ran as straight as an arrow through a flat desert plain covered with scattered clumps of aloe and cactus-like euphorbia.

As the Bedfords headed towards the heat-hazed,

purplish mountains that broke up the horizon, the coconut palms gradually disappeared and the land became more arid, but with a surprisingly wide variety of trees – acacias, tamarisks, jujube and doum palms – breaking up the desert's monotony.

Once they were well away from Aden, out on the open plain, the heat became even worse and was made bearable only by the wind created by the lorries. This wind, however, churned up dense clouds of dust that made most of the men choke and, in some cases, vomit over the rattling tailgates.

'Heave it up over the back,' Jimbo helpfully instructed Ben as he tried to hold his stomach's contents in with pursed lips and bulging cheeks. 'If you do it over the side and that wind blows it back in, over us, you'll have to lick us clean with your furry tongue. So do it over the rear, lad.'

His cheeks deathly white and still bulging, the trooper nodded and threw himself to the back of the vehicle, hanging over the tailgate and vomiting unrestrainedly into the cloud of dust being churned up by the wheels. He was soon followed by his fellow trooper, Taff Thomas, who picked the exact same spot to empty his tortured stomach, while the more experienced men covered their faces with scarves and either practised deep, even breathing or amused themselves with some traditional bullshit.

'Don't worry about it,' Ken said to Taff as the latter wiped his mucky lips clean with a handkerchief and tried to control his heavy breathing. 'You'll feel better after you've had a good nosh at Thumier. Great grub they do there. Raw liver, tripe, runny eggs, oysters, octopus, snails that look like snot, green pea soup . . .'

Taff groaned and went to throw up again over the back of the bouncing, rattling Bedford, into boiling, choking clouds of sand.

'Bet you've never eaten a snail in your life,' Larry said, more loudly than was strictly necessary. 'That's nosh for refined folk.'

'Refined?' Ken replied, glancing sideways as Taff continued heaving over the tailgate. 'What's so refined about pulling a piece of snot out of a shell and letting it slither down your throat? That's puke-making – not refined.'

'Ah, God!' Ben groaned, then covered his mouth with his soiled handkerchief as he shuddered visibly.

'Throw up in that,' Jimbo warned him, 'and I'll make you wipe your face with it. Go and join your friend there.'

Shuddering even more violently, Ben dived for the tailgate, hanging over it beside his heaving friend.

'A little vomit goes a long way,' Ken said. 'Across half of this bloody desert, in fact. I never knew those two had it in 'em. It just goes to show.'

Men in the other Bedfords were suffering in the same way, but the column continued across the desert to where the lower slopes of the mountains, covered in lava, with a mixture of limestone and sand, made for an even rougher, slower ride. Here there were no trees, so no protection from the sun, and when the lorries slowed to practically a crawl – which they had to do repeatedly to navigate the rocky terrain – they filled up immediately with swarms of buzzing flies and whining, biting mosquitoes.

'Shit!' Les complained, swiping frantically at the frantic insects. 'I'm being eaten alive here!'

'Malaria's next on the list,' Ken added. 'That bloody Paludrine's useless.'

'Why the hell doesn't this driver go faster?' Larry asked as he too swatted uselessly at the attacking insects. 'At this rate, we might as well get out and walk.'

'It's the mountains,' Ben explained, feeling better for having emptied his stomach and seemingly oblivious to the insects. 'This road's running across their lower slopes, which are rocky and full of holes.'

'How observant!' Ken exclaimed.

'A bright lad!' Les added.

'Real officer material,' Larry chimed in. 'These bleedin' insects only go for red blood, so his must be blue.'

'I'm never bothered by insects,' Ben confirmed. 'It's odd, but it's true.'

'How's your stomach?' Ken asked the trooper.

'Feeling sick again?' queried Les.

'I can still smell his vomit from an hour ago,' Larry said, 'and it's probably what attracted these bloody insects. They're after his puke.'

Ben and Taff dived simultaneously for the rear of the lorry and started heaving yet again while the others, feeling superior once more, kept swatting at and cursing the insects. This went on until the Bedford bounced down off the slopes and headed across another relatively flat plain of limestone, sandstone and lava fields. They had now been on the Dhala road for two hours, but it seemed longer than that.

Mercifully, after another hour of hellish heat and dust, with the sun even higher in a silvery-white sky, they arrived at the SAS forward base at Thumier, located near the Habilayn airstrip, sixty miles from Aden and just thirty miles from the hostile Yemeni border.

'We could have been flown here!' Ben complained.

'That would have been too easy,' Ken explained. 'For us, *nothing's* made easy.'

In reality the camp was little more than an uninviting collection of tents pitched in a sandy area surrounded by high, rocky ridges where half a dozen SAS observation posts, hidden from view and swept constantly by dust, recced the landscape for enemy troop movements. There were no guards at the camp entrance because there were no gates; nor was there a perimeter fence. However, the base was surrounded by sandbagged gun emplacements raised an equal distance apart in a loose circular shape and nicknamed 'hedgehogs' because they were bristling with 25-pounder guns, 3-inch mortars, and Browning 0.5-inch heavy machine-guns. Though the landscape precluded the use of aeroplanes, a flattened area of desert near one of the hedgehogs was being used as a helicopter landing pad, on which were now parked the camp's helicopters, including a Sikorski S-55 Whirlwind and a British-built Wessex S-58 Mark 1. The Bedfords of A Squadron were lined up near the helicopters. A line of men, mostly from that squadron, all with tin plates and eating utensils, was inching into the largest tent of all – the mess tent – for their evening meal. A modified 4×4 Willys jeep, with armoured perspex screens and a Browning 0.5-inch heavy machine-gun mounted on the front, was parked outside the second largest tent, which was being used as a combined HQ and briefing room. Other medium-sized tents were being used as the quartermaster's store, armoury, NAAFI and surgery. A row of smaller tents located near portable showers and boxed-in, roofless chemical latrines were the make-do 'bashas', or sleeping quarters. Beyond those tents lay the desert.

'Home, sweet fucking home,' Les said in disgust as he clambered out of the Bedford to stand beside his mate Ken and the still shaky troopers, Ben and Taff, in the unrelenting sunlight. 'Welcome to Purgatory!'

Ken turned to Ben and Taff, both of whom were

white as ghosts and wiping sweat from their faces. 'Feel better, do you?' he asked.

'Yes, Corporal,' they both lied.

'The vomiting's always followed by diarrhoea,' Ken helpfully informed them. 'You'll be shitting for days.'

'It rushes out before you can stop it,' Les added. 'As thin as pea soup. It's in your pants before you even know you've done it. A right fucking mess, it makes.'

'Christ!' Ben exclaimed.

'God Almighty!' Taff groaned.

'Keep your religious sentiments to yourselves,' Jimbo admonished them, materializing out of the shimmering heat haze to study them keenly. 'Are you two OK?'

'Yes, Sarge,' they both answered.

'You look a bit shaky.'

'I'm all right, Sarge,' Ben said.

'So am I,' Taff insisted.

'They don't have any insides left,' Ken explained. 'But apart from that, they're perfectly normal.'

Jimbo was too distracted to take in the corporal's little joke. 'Good,' he said. 'So pick up your kit, hump it over to those tents, find yourselves a basha, have a smoko and brew-up, then meet me at the quartermaster's store in thirty minutes precisely. Get to it.'

When Jimbo had marched away, the weary men humped their 60-pound bergens onto their backs, picked up their personal weapons – either 5.56mm M16 assault rifles, 7.62mm L1A1 SLRs or 7.62mm L42A1 bolt-action sniper rifles – and marched across the dusty clearing to the bashas. Because the two new troopers had been placed in their care, Ken and Les were to share a tent with Ben and Taff.

'Well, it isn't exactly the Ritz,' Ken said, leaning forward to keep his head from scraping the roof of the tent, 'but I suppose it'll do.'

'They wouldn't let you into the Ritz,' Les replied, 'if you had the Queen Mother on your arm. This tent is probably more luxurious than anything you've had in your whole life.'

'Before I joined the Army,' Ken replied, swatting uselessly at the swarm of flies and mosquitoes at his face, 'when I was just a lad, I lived in a spacious two-up, two-down that had all the mod cons, including a real toilet in the backyard with a nice bolt and chain.'

'All right, lads,' Les said to Ben and Taff, who were both wiping sweat from their faces, swatting at the flies and mosquitoes, and nervously examining the sandy soil beneath the camp-beds for signs of scorpions or snakes, 'put your bergens down, roll your sleeping bags out on the beds, then let's go to the QM's tent for the rest of our kit.'

'*More* kit?' Ben asked in disbelief as he gratefully lowered his heavy bergen to the ground, recalling that it contained a hollow-fill sleeping bag; a waterproof one-man sheet; a portable hexamine stove with blocks of fuel; an aluminium mess tin, mug and utensils; a brew kit, including sachets of tea, powdered milk and sugar; spare radio batteries; water bottles; extra ammunition; matches and flint; an emergency first-aid kit; signal flares; and various survival aids, including compass, pencil torch and batteries, and even surgical blades and butterfly sutures.

'Dead right,' Les said with a sly grin. '*More* kit. This is just the beginning, kid. Now lay your sleeping bag out and let's get out of here.'

Jimbo and Dead-eye were sharing the adjoining tent with the medical specialist, Larry, leaving the fourth bed free for the eventual return of their squadron signaller, Trooper Terry Malkin. After picking a bed, each man unstrapped his bergen, removed his sleeping bag, rolled it out on the bed, then picked up his weapon and left the tent, to gather with the others outside the quartermaster's store.

'A pretty basic camp,' Jimbo said to Dead-eye as they crossed the hot, dusty clearing.

'It'll do,' Dead-eye replied, glancing about him with what seemed like a lack of interest, though in fact his grey gaze missed nothing.

'Makes no difference to you, does it, Dead-eye? Just another home from home.'

'That's right,' Dead-eye said quietly.

'What do you think of the new men?'

'They throw up too easily. But now that they've emptied their stomachs, they might be OK.'

'They'll be all right with Brooke and Moody?'

'I reckon so.'

The four men under discussion were already gathered together with the rest of the squadron, waiting to collect the balance of their kit. Already concerned about the weight of his bergen, Ben was relieved to discover that the additional kit consisted only of a mosquito net, insect repellent, extra soap, an aluminium wash-basin, a small battery-operated reading lamp for use in the tent, a pair of ankle-length, rubber-soled desert boots, a DPM (disruptive pattern material) cotton shirt and trousers, and an Arab *shemagh* to protect the nose, mouth and eyes from the sun, sand and insects.

'All right,' Jimbo said when the men, still holding their rifles in one hand, somehow managed to gather the new kit up under their free arm and stood awkwardly in the fading light of the sinking sun, 'carry that lot back to your tents, leave it on your bashas, then go off to the mess tent for dinner. Report to the HQ tent for your briefing at seven p.m. sharp . . . Are you deaf? *Get going!*'

Though dazed from heat and exhaustion, the men hurried back through the mercifully cooling dusk to raise their mosquito nets over the camp-beds. This done, they left their kit under the nets and then made their way gratefully to the mess tent. There they had a replenishing meal of 'compo' sausage, mashed potatoes and beans, followed by rice pudding, all washed down with hot tea.

While eating his meal, Les struck up a conversation with Corporal Jamie McBride of A Squadron, who had just returned from one of the OPs located high in the Radfan, the bare, rocky area to the north of Aden.

'What's it like up there?' Les asked.

'Hot, dusty, wind-blown and fart-boring,' McBride replied indifferently.

'Good to get back down, eh?'

'Right,' the corporal said.

'I note we have a NAAFI tent,' Les said, getting to the subject that concerned him the most. 'Anything in it?'

'Beer and cigarettes,' the weary McBride replied.

'Anything else?'

'Blue magazines and films, whores, whips and chains . . . What do *you* think?'

'Just asking, mate. Sorry.'

Realizing that his fellow soldier was under some stress, Les gulped down the last of his hot tea, waved his hand in farewell, then followed the others out of the mess tent.

'Another fucking briefing,' he complained to Ken as they crossed the clearing to the big HQ tent. 'I need it like a hole in the head.'

'You've already got that,' his mate replied. 'Between one ear and the other there's nothing but a great big empty space.'

'Up yours an' all,' said Les wearily.

2

The men were briefed by their Commanding Officer, Lieutenant-Colonel Patrick 'Paddy' Callaghan, with whom most of them had recently served in Borneo and who was now on his last tour of duty. Wearing his SAS beret with winged-dagger badge, in DPM trousers, desert boots and a long-sleeved cotton shirt, Callaghan was standing on a crude wooden platform, in the large, open-ended HQ tent, in front of a blackboard covered with a map of Yemen. Seated on wooden chairs on the platform were his second in command, Major Timothy Williamson, and the Squadron Commander, Captain Ellsworth. The members of D Squadron were in four rows of metal chairs in front of Callaghan, their backs turned to the opening of the tent, which, as evening fell, allowed a cooling breeze to blow in.

Outside, a Sikorski S-55 Whirlwind was coming in to land before last light, the noise of Bedfords and jeeps was gradually tapering off, NCOs were bawling their last instructions of the day at their troops and Arab workers, and the 25-pounders in the hedgehogs around the perimeter were firing their practice rounds, as they did every evening.

It was a lot of noise to talk against, but after the usual introductory bullshit between himself and his impatient, frisky squadron of SAS troopers, Lieutenant-Colonel Callaghan knuckled down to the business at hand, only stopping periodically to let some noise from outside fade away.

'I might as well be blunt with you,' he began. 'What we're fighting for here is a lost cause created by our lords and masters, who are attempting to leave the colony while retaining a presence here at the same time. Most of you men are experienced enough from similar situations to know that this is impossible, but it's the situation we've inherited and we're stuck with it.'

'We're always stuck with it,' Les said. 'They ram it to us right up the backside and expect us to live with it.'

'Who?' Ben asked, looking puzzled.

'Politicians,' the lance-corporal replied. 'Our lords and masters.'

'All right, you men,' Jimbo said in a voice that sounded like a torrent of gravel. 'Shut up and let Lieutenant-Colonel Callaghan speak.'

'Sorry, boss,' Les said.

'So,' Callaghan continued, 'a bit of necessary historical background.' This led to the customary moans and groans, which the officer endured for a moment, before gesturing for silence. 'I know you don't like it, but it's necessary, so please pay attention.' When they had settled down, he continued: 'A trade centre since antiquity, Aden came under the control of the Turks in the sixteenth century. We Brits established ourselves here by treaty in 1802, used it as a coaling station on the sea route to India, and made it a crown colony in 1937. Because it is located at the southern entrance to the Red Sea, between Arabia and eastern and north-eastern Africa, its main function has always been as a commercial centre for neighbouring states, as well as a refuelling stop for ships. However, it really gained political and commercial importance after the opening of the Suez canal in 1869 and in the present century as a result of the development of the rich oilfields in Arabia and the Persian Gulf. In 1953 an oil refinery was built at Little Aden, on the west side of the bay. Aden became partially self-governing in 1962 and was incorporated into the Federation of South Arabia, the FSA, in 1963, which is when its troubles began.'

Callaghan stopped to take a breath and ensure that he had the men's full attention. Though the usual bored expressions were in evidence, they were all bearing with him.

'Opposition to the British presence here began with the abortive Suez operation of 1956, increased with the emergence of Nasserism via the inflammatory broadcasts of Radio Cairo, and reached its high point with the so-called shotgun marriage of the FSA of 1959–63. This, by the way, linked the formerly feudal sheikdoms lying between Yemen and the coast with the urban area of Aden Colony. Steadily mounting antagonism towards our presence here was in no way eased by the establishment in 1960 of our Middle East Command Headquarters.'

Stopping momentarily to let a recently landed Sikorski whine into silence, Callaghan glanced out through the tent's opening and saw a troop of heavily armed soldiers of the Parachute Regiment marching towards the airstrip, from where they were to fly by Wessex to the mountains of the Radfan. Having served in Malaya and Borneo, Callaghan had a particular fondness for the jungle, but not the desert. Nevertheless, the sight of that darkening, dust-covered ground guarded by hedgehogs bristling with 25-pounders, mortars and machine-guns brought back fond memories of his earliest days with the Regiment in North Africa in 1941. That war had been something of a schoolboy's idea of adventure, with its daring raids in Land Rovers and on foot; this war, though also in desert, albeit mountainous, would be considerably less romantic and more vicious.

'In September 1962,' the CO continued when silence had returned, 'the hereditary ruler of Yemen, the Imam, was overthrown in a left-wing, Army-led coup. This coup was consolidated almost immediately with the arrival of Egyptian troops. The new republican government in Yemen then called on its brothers in the occupied south – in other words, Aden and the Federation – to prepare for revolution and join it in the battle against colonialism. What this led to, in fact, was an undeclared war between two colonial powers – Britain against a Soviet-backed Egypt – with the battleground being the barren, mountainous territory lying between the Gulf of Aden and Saudi Arabia.'

'Is that where we'll be fighting?' Ken asked.

'Most of you in the Radfan; a few in the streets of Aden itself. Aden, however, will be covered in a separate briefing.'

'Right, boss.'

'Initial SAS involvement in this affair took place, with discreet official backing from Whitehall, over the next eight years or so, when the royalist guerrilla army of the deposed Imam was aided by the Saudis and strengthened by the addition of a mercenary force composed largely of SAS veterans. Operating out of secret bases in the Aden Federation, they fought two campaigns simultaneously. On the one hand they were engaged in putting down a tribal uprising in the Radfan, adjoining Yemen; on the other, they were faced with their first battle against highly organized urban terrorism in Aden itself.'

'That's a good one!' Ken said. 'In the mountains of Yemen, a team of SAS veterans becomes part of a guerrilla force. Meanwhile, in Aden, only a few miles south, their SAS mates are suppressing a guerrilla campaign.'

'We are nothing if not versatile,' Callaghan replied urbanely.

'Dead right about that, boss.'

'May I continue?'

'Please do, boss.'

'In July this year Harold Macmillan set 1968 as the year for the Federation's self-government, promising that independence would be accompanied by a continuing British presence in Aden. In short, we wouldn't desert the tribal leaders with whom we'd maintained protection treaties since the last century.'

'However, Egyptian, Yemeni and Adeni nationalists are still bringing weapons, land-mines and explosives across the border. At the same time, the border tribesmen, who view guerrilla warfare as a way of life, are being supplied with money and weapons by Yemen. The engaged battle is for control of the ferociously hot Radfan mountains. There is practically no water there, and no roads at all.'

'But somehow or other,' Dead-eye noted, 'the war is engaged there.'

'Correct. The Emergency was declared in December 1963. Between then and the arrival of A Squadron in April of that year, an attempt to subdue the Radfan was made by a combined force

36

of three Federal Regular Army battalions of Arabs, supported by British tanks, guns and engineers. As anticipated by those who understood the tribal mentality, it failed. True, the FRA battalions did manage to occupy parts of the mountains for a few weeks at a cost of five dead and twelve wounded. Once they withdrew, however – as they had to sooner or later, to go back to the more important task of guarding the frontier – the patient tribesmen returned to their former hill positions and immediately began attacking military traffic on the Dhala Road linking Yemen and Aden – the same road that brought you to this camp.'

'An unforgettable journey!' Ken whispered.

'Diarrhoea and vomit every minute for three hours,' Les replied. 'Will we ever forget it?'

'While they were doing so,' said Callaghan, having heard neither man, 'both Cairo and the Yemeni capital of Sana were announcing the FRA's withdrawal from the Radfan as a humiliating defeat for the imperialists.'

'In other words, we got what we deserved.'

'Quite so, Corporal Brooke.' Though smiling, Callaghan sighed as if weary. 'Given this calamity, the Federal government . . .'

'Composed of . . .?' Dead-eye interjected.

'Tribal rulers and Adeni merchants,' the CO explained.

'More A-rabs,' Ken said. 'Got you, boss.'

'The Federal government then asked for more military aid from the British, who, despite their own severe doubts – believing, correctly, that this would simply make matters worse – put together a mixed force of brigade strength, including a squadron each of RAF Hawker Hunter ground-support aircraft, Shackleton bombers, Twin Pioneer transports and roughly a dozen helicopters. Their task was twofold. First, to bring sufficient pressure to bear on the Radfan tribes and prevent the revolt from spreading. Second, to stop the attacks on the Dhala Road. In doing this, they were not to deliberately fire on areas containing women and children; they were not to shell, bomb or attack villages without dropping leaflets warning the inhabitants and telling them to move out. Once the troops came under fire, however, retaliation could include maximum force.'

'Which gets us back to the SAS,' Dead-eye said.

'Yes, Sergeant. Our job is to give back-up to A Squadron in the Radfan. To this end, we'll start with a twenty-four-hour proving patrol, which will also act as your introduction to the area.'

'We don't need an introduction,' the reckless Corporal Brooke said. 'Just send us up there.'

'You *need* an introduction,' Callaghan insisted. 'You're experienced troopers, I agree, but your experience so far has always been in the jungle – first Malaya, then Borneo. You need experience in desert and jungle navigation and that's what you'll get on this proving patrol. We're talking about pure desert of the kind we haven't worked in since the Regiment was formed in 1941, which excludes most of those present in this tent. Desert as hot as North Africa, but even more difficult because it's mountainous. Limestone, sandstone and igneous rocks. Sand and silt. Lava fields and volcanic remains, criss-crossed with deep wadis. The highland plateau, or *kawr*, has an average height of 6500 feet and peaks rising to 8000 to 9000 feet. The plateau itself is broken up by deep valleys or canyons, as well as the wadis. In short, the terrain is hellishly difficult and presents many challenges.'

'Any training before we leave?' Dead-eye asked.

'Yes. One full day tomorrow. Lay up tonight, kitting out and training tomorrow, then move out at last light the same day. The transport will be 4×4 Bedford three-tonners and Saladin armoured cars equipped with 5.56-inch Bren guns. Enjoy your evening off, gentlemen. That's it. Class dismissed.'

Not wanting to waste a minute of their free time, the men hurried out of the briefing room and raced each other to the makeshift NAAFI canteen at the other side of the camp, where they enjoyed a lengthy booze-up of ice-cold bottled beer. Few went to bed sober.

3

Rudely awakened at first light by Jimbo, whose roar could split mountains, the men rolled out of their bashas, quickly showered and shaved, then hurried through the surprisingly cold morning air, in darkness streaked with rising sunlight, to eat as much as they could in fifteen minutes and return to their sleeping quarters.

Once by their beds, and already kitted out, they had only to collect their bergens, kit and weapons, then hurry back out into the brightening light and cross the clearing, through a gentle, moaning wind and spiralling clouds of dust, to the column of Bedfords and Saladins in the charge of still sleepy drivers from the Royal Corps of Transport. The RCT drivers drank hot tea from vacuum flasks and smoked while the SAS men, heavily burdened with their bergens and other kit, clambered up into the back of the lorries. Meanwhile, the sun was rising like a pomegranate over the distant Radfan, casting an exotic, blood-red light through the shadows on the lower slopes of the mountains, making them look more mysterious than dangerous.

'We should be up there in OPs,' Les complained as they settled into their bench seats in the back of a Bedford. 'Not wasting our bleedin' time with a training jaunt.'

'I don't think we're wasting our time,' Ken replied. 'I believe the boss. All our practical experience has been in Borneo and that won't help us here.'

'I wish *I'd* been in Borneo,' Ben said. 'I bet it was more exotic than this dump.'

'It was,' Larry said ironically. 'Steaming jungle, swamps, raging rivers, snakes, scorpions, lizards, giant spiders, fucking dangerous wild pigs, and head-hunting aboriginals blowing poison darts. Join the SAS and see the world – always travelling first class, of course.'

'At least here we've only got flies and mosquitoes,' Taff said hopefully, swatting the first of the morning's insects from his face.

'*Plus* desert snakes, scorpions, centipedes, stinging hornets, spiders and Arab guerrillas who give you no quarter. Make the most of it!'

Having silenced the new men and given them something to think about, Les grinned sadistically at Ken, then glanced out of the uncovered truck as the Saladin in the lead roared into life. Taking this as their cue, the RCT drivers in the Bedfords switched on their ignition, one after the other, and revved the engines in neutral to warm them up. When the last had done the same, the rearmost Saladin followed suit and the column was ready to move. The Bedfords and the Saladin acting as 'Tail-end Charlie' followed the first armoured car out of the camp, throwing up a column of billowing dust as they headed out into the desert.

The route was through an area scattered with coconut and doum palms, acacias, tall ariatas and tamarisks, the latter looking prettily artificial with their feathery branches. They were, however, few and far between. For the most part, the Bedfords bounced and rattled over parched ground strewn with potholes and stones until, about half an hour later, they arrived at an area bounded by a horseshoe-shaped mountain range. The RCT drivers took the Bedfords up the lower slopes as far as they would go, then stopped to let the men out.

The soldiers were lowering their kit to the ground and clambering down when they saw for the first time that one of the Bedfords had brought up a collection of heavier support weapons, including a 7.62mm GPMG (general-purpose machine-gun), a 7.62mm LMG (light machine-gun) and two 51mm mortars.

'Looks like we're in for a pretty long day,' Les muttered ominously.

'No argument about that,' Ken whispered back at him.

When the Bedfords had turned around and headed back the way they had come, Jimbo gathered his men around him. Dead-eye was standing beside him, holding his L42A1 bolt-action sniper rifle and looking as granite-faced as always.

'The Bedfords,' Jimbo said, 'will come back just before last light. Until then we work.' Pausing to let his words sink in, he waved his hands at the heavy weapons piled up to his left. 'As you can see, we've brought along a nice collection of support weapons. We're going to hike up to the summit of this hill and take that lot with us. I hope you're all feeling fit.' The men moaned and groaned melodramatically, but Jimbo, his crooked lip curling, waved them into silence. 'For most of you,' he said, 'your previous practical experience was in jungle or swamp. A few of us have had experience in the African desert, but even that didn't involve anything like these mountains. You are here, therefore, to adapt to a terrain of mountainous desert, with all that entails.'

'What's that, Sarge?' Ben asked innocently.

'Wind and sand. Potentially damaging dips and holes covered by sand, soil or shrubs. Loose gravel and wind-smoothed, slippery rocks. Ferocious heat. All in all, it calls for a wide variety of survival skills of the kind you haven't so far acquired.' He cast a quick grin at the impassive Dead-eye, then turned back to the men. 'And the first lesson,' he continued, nodding at the summit of the ridge, 'is to get up there, carrying the support weapons and your own kit.' Glancing up automatically, the men were not reassured by what they saw. 'It's pretty steep,' Jimbo said. 'It's also covered with sharp and loose stones. Be careful you don't break an ankle or trip and roll down. And watch out for snakes, scorpions and the like. Even when not poisonous, some of them can inflict a nasty bite . . . So, let's get to it.'

He jabbed his finger at various groups, telling them which weapons and components they were to carry between them. Corporal Ken Brooke, Lance-Corporal Les Moody, and Troopers Ben Riley and Taff Thomas were assigned as the four-man GPMG team. Lance-Corporal Larry Johnson, already burdened with his extra medical kit, got off scot-free.

'We picked the wrong specialist training,' Les complained. 'Johnson gets off with everything.'

'It's not *just* the fact that I'm our medical specialist,' Larry replied, beaming smugly. 'It's because I have charm and personality. It comes natural, see.'

'So does farting from your mouth,' Ken shot back. 'Come on, Les, let's hump this thing.'

The four men tossed for it. Ken lost and became number two: the one who had to hump the GPMG onto his shoulders. Sighing, he unlocked the front legs of the 30lb steel tripod, swung them forward into the high-mount position and relocked them. Then, with Les's assistance, he hauled the tripod up onto his shoulders with the front legs resting on his chest and the rear one trailing backwards over his equally heavy bergen. With the combined weight of the steel tripod, ammunition belts of 7.62mm rounds, and rucksack adding up to 130lb, Ken felt exhausted before he had even started.

'You look like a bleedin' elephant,' Les informed

him. 'I just hope you're as strong.'

'Go fuck yourself,' Ken barked back.

The four-way toss had made Les the gun controller, Ben the observer and Taff the number one, or trigger man. Between them, apart from personal gear, they had to carry two spare barrels weighing 6lb each, a spare return spring, a dial sight, marker pegs, two aiming posts, an aiming lamp, a recoil buffer, a tripod sighting bracket, a spare-parts wallet, and the gun itself.

'This doesn't look easy,' Ben said, glancing nervously up the steep, rocky slope as Les distributed the separate parts of the GPMG.

'It's a fucking sight easier than humping that tripod,' Les informed him, 'so count yourself lucky.'

'Move out!' Jimbo bawled.

The whole squad moved out in single file, spread well apart as they would be on a real patrol, with the men who were carrying the support weapons leaning forward even more than the others. The climb was both backbreaking and dangerous, for each man was forced to navigate the steep slope while looking out for sharp or loose stones that could either break an ankle or roll from under his feet, sending him tumbling back down the mountain. In this, they were helped neither by the sheer intensity of the heat nor the growing swarms of buzzing flies and whining mosquitoes attracted by their copious sweat.

Almost driven mad by the mosquitoes, the men's attempts to swat them away came as near to unbalancing them as did the loose, rolling stones. More than one man found himself suddenly twisting sideways, dragged down by his own kit or support weapon, after he had swung his hand too violently at his tormentors. Saved by the helping hand of the man coming up behind him, he might then find himself stepping on a loose stone, which would roll like a log beneath him, sending him violently forwards or backwards; or he would start slipping on loose gravel as it slid away underfoot.

By now the breathing of every man was agonized and not helped by the fact that the air was filled with the dust kicked up by their boots or the tumbling stones and sliding gravel. The dust hung around them in clouds, making them choke and cough, and limiting visibility to a dangerous degree, eventually reducing the brightening sunlight to a distant, silvery haze. To make matters worse, each man's vision was even more blurred when his own stinging sweat ran into his eyes.

The climb of some 1500 feet took them two

hellish hours but led eventually to the summit of the ridge. This had different, more exotic trees scattered here and there along its otherwise rocky, parched, relatively flat ground, and overlooked a vast plain of sand, silt and polished lava.

Throwing themselves gratefully to the ground, the men were about to open their water bottles when Jimbo stopped them. 'No,' he said. 'Put those bottles away.'

'But, Sarge . . .' Taff began in disbelief.

'Shut up and listen to me,' Jimbo replied. 'As you've all just discovered, the heat in the mountains can wring the last drop of sweat out of you much quicker than you can possibly imagine — no matter how fit you are. If you allow this to happen, you'll soon be dehydrated, exhausted, and if you don't get water in time, dead of thirst.'

'So let us drink our water,' Les said, shaking his bottle invitingly.

'No,' the sergeant replied. 'Your minimum daily intake of water should be two gallons a day, but on a real operation we won't be able to resup by chopper because this would give away the position of the OP. For this reason, you'll have to learn to conserve the water you carry inside your body by minimal movement during the day, replenishing your water bottles each night by sneaking down to the nearest stream.'

'So we should ensure that the OP site is always near a stream,' Ben said, 'and not on top of a high ridge or mountain like this.'

'Unfortunately, no. It's because they're aware of the constant need for water that the rebel tribesmen always check the areas around streams for our presence. Therefore, the site for your OP should be chosen for the view it gives of enemy supply routes, irrespective of its proximity to water. You then go out at night and search far and wide for your water, no matter how difficult or dangerous that task may be.'

'Sounds like a right pain to me,' Ken said.

'It is. I should point out here, to make you feel even worse — but to make you even more careful — that even after dark the exertion of foraging for water can produce a dreadful thirst that can make you consume half of what you collect on the way back. In short, these mountains make the jungles of Borneo seem like sheer luxury. And that's no exaggeration, believe me.'

'I believe you,' Les said, still clutching his water bottle. 'Can I have a drink now?'

'No. That water has to last until tonight and you've only brought one bottle each.'

'But we're all dying of thirst,' Ken complained.

Jimbo pointed to the trees scattered sparsely along the otherwise parched summit of the ridge. 'That,' he said, indicating a tree covered in a plum-like fruit, 'is the jujube. Its fruit is edible and will also quench your thirst . . . And those,' he continued, pointing to the bulbous plants hanging from the branches of a tree that looked like a cactus, 'are euphorbia. If you pierce them with a knife, or slice the top off, you'll find they contain a drinkable juice that's a bit like milk.'

'So when *can* we drink our water?' Taff pleaded.

'When you've put up your bashas, cleaned and checked your weapons, put in a good morning's firing practice and are eating your scran. Meanwhile, you can eat and drink from those trees.'

'Bashas?' Ken glanced down the slopes of the ridge at the barren, sunlit plain below, running out for miles to more distant mountains. 'What are we putting bashas up for? We're only here for one day.'

'They're to let you rest periodically from the sun and keep you from getting sunstroke. So just make triangular shelters with your poncho sheets. Now get to it.'

The men constructed their triangular shelters by standing two upright sticks with Y-shaped tops about six feet apart, running a length of taut cord between them, draping the poncho sheet over the cord, with one short end, about 18 inches long, facing away from the sun and the other running obliquely all the way to the ground, forming a solid wall. Both sides of the poncho sheet were then made secure by the strings stitched into them and tied to wooden pegs hammered into the soil. Dried grass and bracken were then strewn on the ground inside the 'tent' and finally the sleeping bag was rolled out to make a crude but effective mattress.

When the bashas had been constructed, the men were allowed to rest from the sun for fifteen minutes. Though it was still not yet nine a.m. local time, the sun's heat was already intense.

Once rested, the men were called out to dismantle, clean of dust and sand, oil and reassemble the weapons, a task which, with the dust blowing continuously, was far from easy. Jimbo then made them set the machine-guns up on the ridge and aim at specific targets on the lower slopes of the hill: mostly clumps of parched shrubs and trees. The rest of the morning was spent in extensive practice with the support weapons, first using the tripods, then firing both the heavy GPMG and the LMG from the hip with the aid of a sling.

The GPMG, in particular, had a violent backblast that almost punched some of the men off their feet. But in the end they all managed to hold it and hit their targets when standing. The noise of the machine-guns was shocking in the desert silence and reverberated eerily around the encircling mountains.

Two hours later, when weapons practice was over, the men were again made to dismantle, clean, oil and reassemble the weapons, which were then wrapped in cloth to protect them from the dust and sand. By now labouring beneath an almost overhead sun, the men were soaked in sweat, sunburnt and gasping with thirst, and so were given another ten-minute break, which they spent in their bashas, sipping water and drawing greedily on cigarettes. The break over, they were called out again, this time by the fearsome Sergeant Parker, for training with their personal weapons.

Dead-eye's instruction included not only the firing of the weapons, at which he was faultless, but the art of concealment on exposed ridges, scrambling up and down the slopes on hands and elbows, rifle held horizontally across the face. The posture adopted for this strongly resembled the 'leopard crawl' used for the crossing of the dreaded entrails ditch during 'Sickener One' at Bradbury Lines, Hereford. It was less smelly here, but infinitely more dangerous than training in Britain, as the men had to crawl over sharp, burning-hot rocks that could not only cut skin and break bones, but also could be hiding snakes, scorpions or poisonous spiders.

More than one man was heard to cry out and jump up in shock as he came across something hideous on the ground where he was crawling. But he was shouted back down by the relentless Jimbo, who was always watching on the sidelines as Dead-eye led them along the ridge on their bellies.

'Is that what you'd do if you were under fire?' Jimbo would bawl. 'See a spider and jump up like an idiot to get shot to pieces? Get your face back in the dirt, man, and don't get up again until I tell you!'

While some of the men resented having firing practice when most of them had not only done it all before but had even been blooded in real combat, what they were in fact learning was how to deal with an unfamiliar terrain. Dead-eye also taught them how to time their shots for when the constantly swirling dust and sand had blown away long enough for them to get a clear view of the target. Finally, they were learning to fire accurately into the sunlight by estimating the position of the target by its shadow, rather than by trying to look directly at it. By lunchtime, when they had mastered this new skill, they were thoroughly exhausted and, in many cases, bloody and bruised from the sharp, burning rocks. They were suffering no less from the many bites inflicted by the whining mosquitoes.

'I look like a bleedin' leper,' Ben complained as he rubbed more insect repellent over his badly bitten wrists, hands and face, 'with all these disgusting mosquito bites.'

'Not as bad as leeches,' Les informed him smugly as he sat back, ignoring his mosquito bites, to have a smoko. 'Those little buggers sucked us dry in Borneo. Left us bloodless.'

'By the time they finish with us,' Taff said, 'you could throw us in a swamp filled with leeches and they'd all die of thirst. I'm fucking bloodless, I tell you!'

In the relative cool of his poncho tent, Ken removed his water bottle from his mouth, licked his lips, then lay back with his hands behind his head and closed his eyes.

'If you go to sleep you'll feel like hell when you wake up,' Larry solemnly warned him.

'I'm not sleeping,' Ken replied. 'I'm just resting my eyes. They get tired from the sunlight.'

'Getting hotter and brighter every minute,' Larry said. 'It'll soon be like hell out there.'

'We'll all get there eventually,' Les told him, 'so we'd better get used to it.'

'Amen to that,' Ken said.

Immediately after lunch they rolled out of the shade of their bashas to return to the baking oven of the ridge, where, although dazzled by the brilliance of the sky, they took turns to set up, fire and dismantle the 51mm mortar. It weighed a mere 13lb, had no sophisticated sights or firing mechanism, and was essentially just a simple tube with a fixed base plate. Conveniently, it could be carried over the shoulder with its ammunition distributed among the rest of the patrol. The user had only to wedge the base plate into the ground, hold the tube at the correct angle for the estimated range, then drop a bomb into the top of the tube. Though first-shot accuracy was relatively difficult with such a crude weapon, a skilled operator could zero in on a target with a couple of practice shots, then fire up to eight accurate rounds a minute. Most of the men were managing to do this within the first hour, and were gratified to see the explosions tearing up the flat plain below, forming spectacular columns of spiralling smoke, sand and dust.

Even though they had protected their faces with their *shemaghs*, they were badly burnt by the sun, on the road to dehydration, and very close to complete exhaustion when, in the late afternoon, Jimbo and Dead-eye called a halt to the weapons training and said they would now hike back down the hill to the waiting Bedfords.

Believing they were about to return to the base camp, the men enthusiastically packed up their bashas, humped the support weapons back onto their bruised shoulders, strapped their heavy bergens to their backs, picked up their personal weapons and hiked in single file back down the hill. If anything, this was even more dangerous than the uphill climb, for they were now growing dizzy with exhaustion and were forced to hike in the direction of the sliding gravel and stones, which tended to make the descent dangerously fast. Luckily, they were close to the bottom when the first man, Taff, let out a yelp as the gravel slid under his feet, sending him backwards into the dirt, to roll the rest of the way down in a billowing cloud of dust and sand. He was picking himself up when two others followed the same way, either tripping or sliding on loose gravel, then losing their balance before rolling down the hill. The rest of the group managed to make it down without incident, though by now all of them were utterly exhausted and soaking in sweat.

'Right,' Dead-eye said. 'Hump those support weapons back up onto the Bedford, then gather around me and Sergeant Ashman.

The men did as they were told, then tried to get their breath back while wiping the sweat from their faces and, in some cases, vainly trying to wring their shirts and trousers dry. They were still breathing painfully and scratching their many insect bites when they gathered around the two sergeants.

Any hopes they might have held of heading back to the relative comforts of the base camp were dashed when Jimbo gave them a lecture on desert navigation, much of it based on his World War Two experiences with the Long Range Desert Group. The lecture took an hour and, to the men's dismay, included a hike of over a mile, fully kitted, out into the blazing-hot desert. This was for the purpose of demonstrating how to measure distance by filling one trouser pocket with small stones and transferring a stone from that pocket to the other after each hundred steps.

'The average pace,' Jimbo explained, 'is 30 inches, so each stone represents approximately 83 yards. So if you lose your compass or, as is just as likely, simply have no geographical features by which to assess distance, you can easily calculate the distance you're marching or have marched by multiplying the number of stones transferred by eighty-three. That gives the distance in yards.'

Though the exhausted men had been forced to walk all this distance in the burning, blinding sunlight, they had been followed by one of the Bedfords. Fondly imagining that this had come out to take them back, they had their hopes dashed again when some small shovels, a couple of radios and various pieces of wiring were handed down to them by the driver.

Jimbo and Dead-eye, both seemingly oblivious to the heat, then took turns at showing the increasingly shattered men how to scrape shallow lying-up positions, or LUPs, out of the sand and check them for buried scorpions or centipedes. Dead-eye was in charge of this particular lesson and, when he had finished scraping out his own demonstration LUP, he made the exhausted men do the same, kicking the sand back into the scrapes when they failed to do it correctly and making them start all over again. When one of the men collapsed during this exercise, the inscrutable sergeant patiently aroused him by splashing cold water on his face, then made him complete his scrape, which amazingly the man did, swaying groggily in the heat.

A short break was allowed for a limited intake of water, then Jimbo gave them a lesson in special desert signalling, covering Morse code, special codes and call-sign signals; use of the radios and how to clean them of sand; recognition of radio 'black spots' caused by the peculiar atmospheric conditions of the mountainous desert; setting up standard and makeshift antennas; and the procedure for calling in artillery fire and air strikes, which would be their main task when in their OPs in the Radfan.

Most of the men were already rigid with exhaustion, dehydration and mild sunstroke when Jimbo took another thirty minutes to show them how to make an improvised compass by variously stroking a sewing needle in one direction against a piece of silk and suspending it in a loop of thread so that it pointed north; by laying the needle on a piece of paper or bark and floating it on water in a cup or mess tin; or by stropping a razor-blade against the palm of the hand and, as with the sewing needle, suspending it from a piece of thread to point north.

Mercifully, the sun was starting to sink when he showed them various methods of purifying and conserving water; then, finally, how to improvise water-filtering systems and crude cookers out of old oil drums and biscuit tins.

'And that's it,' he said, studying their glazed faces with thinly veiled amusement. 'Your long day in the desert is done. Now it's back to base camp.'

'Which you can only do,' Dead-eye told them, 'if you manage to leg it back to the Bedfords.'

'Aw, Jesus!' Larry said without thinking. 'Can't we all pile into *that* Bedford and let it take us back to the others?'

'That Bedford is for the equipment only,' Dead-eye told him. 'Besides, you men have to get used to the desert, and this last hike is all part of your training. Now get going.'

Relieved, at least, of the heavy support weapons, the men heaved their packed bergens and other kit onto their aching backs, turned to face the sinking sun, and walked in a daze back to the other Bedfords. Two almost collapsed on the way and had to be helped by the others, which slowed them down considerably; but just before last light they all made it and practically fell into the trucks, which bounced and rattled every yard of the half-hour journey back to the camp.

Battered and bruised, covered in insect bites, smeared with sweat-soaked sand and dust, hungry and unbelievably thirsty, they collapsed on their steel beds in the tents and could hardly rouse themselves even to shower, shave and head off to the mess tent. Indeed, most of them were still lying there, almost catatonic, when Jimbo did a round of the tents, bawling repeatedly that those not seen having a decent meal would be RTU'd – returned to their original unit. Though they all cursed the SAS, so great was the shame attaching to this fate that they rolled off their beds, attended to their ablutions, dressed in clean clothes and marched on aching legs to the mess tent to have their scran and hot tea. Somewhat restored, they then made for the NAAFI tent to get drunk on cold beer. Finally, after what seemed like the longest day of their lives, they surrendered to sleep like children.

4

The men began their proving patrol the following evening, loading up the Bedfords just before last light with their individual kit and support weapons. For their personal weapons, old Borneo hands like Ken Brooke and Les Moody still favoured the M16 5.56mm assault rifle, which accepted a bayonet and could fire a variety of grenades although it was not so good in desert conditions because of its poor long-range accuracy and tendency to jam up with sand.

Dead-eye, said to be the best shot in the Regiment, preferred the L42A1 7.62mm bolt-action sniper rifle, which had a telescopic sight, was robust and reliable, and had good stopping power at long range, making it ideal for sniping from high mountain ridges. While some of the other men likewise favoured this weapon, most of them had been issued with the L1A1 SLR, which had a twenty-round box magazine, could be used on single shot or automatic, and was notable for its long-range accuracy.

The support weapons included the 7.62mm GPMG; the L4A4 LMG, which was actually a Bren gun modified to accommodate the 7.62mm round; the 51mm mortar with base plate, its ammunition distributed among the men; and a couple of US M79 grenade-launchers, which could be fired from the shoulder. All of these weapons were hauled up into the back of the Bedfords, then followed in by the men, making for very cramped conditions.

'Here we go again,' Larry said, moving his head to avoid the A41 tactical radio set being swung into a more comfortable position on the shoulders of the operator, Lance-Corporal Derek Dickerson. 'Another luxurious journey on the Orient Express!'

'It's nice to have these paid holidays,' Ben said, twisting sideways to avoid being hit by Larry's shoulder-slung wooden medical box. 'It makes me feel so important.'

As the men tried to find comfortable positions on the benches along the sides of the lorries, the sun was sinking low over the distant mountains, casting a blood-red light through the shadows. At the same time, a Sikorski S-55 Whirlwind was roaring into life on the nearby landing pad, whipping up billowing clouds of dust as it prepared to lift off.

'Where the fuck is *he* going?' Les asked in his usual peevish way as he settled into his bench seat in the back of the Bedford.

'The RAF airstrip at Habilayn,' answered Ken. 'It's only a couple of minutes by chopper from here.'

'If it's so close,' Taff asked, 'why couldn't we be flown to the drop zone instead of going by lorry, which will take a lot longer?'

'And make you throw up,' Larry chuckled.

'Ha, ha,' Taff retorted, now used to their bullshit and also determined never to throw up again.

'Because the DZ overlooks an Arab village,' Ken explained, 'and an insertion by chopper would be seen by every rebel in the area.'

'Besides,' Larry added sardonically, 'an insertion by chopper would be too *easy*. We have to do it the *hard* way.'

Nodding their agreement, united by their pride, the men all glanced out from the uncovered Bedford as the lead Saladin roared into life. Taking this as their cue, as they had done the day before, the RCT drivers revved up with a frightful din. When the last of the Bedfords had done the same, the column moved off.

Even as the first Saladin was starting forward, the Whirlwind which had taken off a few minutes earlier was descending towards the horizon in the opposite direction, clearly heading for Habilayn.

'They have it fucking easy,' Les said, meaning the RAF pilots. 'Sitting on their fat arses on soft seats, well out of range of enemy fire. A cushy life, those bastards have.'

'I wouldn't say that,' Ken replied. 'A hell of a lot of them get shot out of the skies. They certainly lost a good few choppers and their crews in Malaya and Borneo.'

'Yeah,' Les agreed grudgingly. 'I just wish I was up there right now, instead of in this bloody lorry.'

'I'd rather be in a Bedford than in a chopper,' Larry said with conviction. 'They're death-traps. At least we can get out and run, which gives you some kind of chance.'

'A really heartening conversation we're having here,' Ken said with a crooked grin. 'If you can say any more to boost our morale, I'd be delighted to hear it.'

'Our Father, which art in heaven . . .' Les began.
'Go shove it!' Ken said, laughing.

The column followed the same route it had taken
the previous day, heading along the Dhala Road,
first passing between rows of handsome coconut
and doum palms, then past more thinly scattered
acacias, ariatas and tamarisks, all of which looked
too pretty to be real. After thinning out gradually, the trees eventually disappeared altogether,
vapourizing into the starlit dusk over an immense,
flat plain in which nothing of interest could be seen,
other than the darkening mountains towards which
they were heading.

The patrol eventually came to the area bounded
by a horseshoe-shaped mountain range where, the
previous day, they had suffered so much, but this
time they did not stop. Instead they kept going
until, a good two hours later, now mercifully in
the cool of the moonlit evening, they arrived at
the lower slopes of the mountains of the Radfan.
There the column of vehicles ground to a halt and
formed a defensive laager, with the 76mm QF guns
and .30-inch machine-guns of the Saladins covering
opposite directions.

The laager completed, the SAS troops disem-
barked, adjusted their webbing and the shoulder

straps of their bergens, then picked up their weapons and fell into a diamond formation that was spread out across the lower slopes of the mountains, away from the laager. Preferred by the SAS in open country and on 'tabs' by night, this marching formation combined the best features of both file and single-file formations, allowing maximum fire-power to be focused on the front. At the same time, as with the other formations, it was designed to give ample protection to the rear and both sides as well.

Dead-eye, nominally the patrol commander, or PC, had chosen to be well out on point, as lead scout, covering the arc of fire immediately in front of the patrol. Jimbo, his fellow sergeant and second in command, or 2IC, was bringing up the rear as Tail-end Charlie, regularly swinging around to face the opposite direction to that in which the men were marching, covering the arc of fire to the rear and ensuring that the patrol had no blind spots. Lance-Corporal Derek Dickerson, humping the all-important A41 tactical radio, was well protected in the middle of the file. The other men, well strung out, were covering firing arcs to the left and right. While Dead-eye and Jimbo had the most demanding jobs, the other men also suffered great stress, because of the need for constant vigilance during the hike.

Dead-eye as PC and Jimbo as 2IC were both compelled to carry items additional to their normal kit, including more detailed maps, navigational equipment, passive night-vision goggles (PNGs), a spare short-range radio, and a SARBE (surface-to-air rescue beacon) for emergency communication with support or extraction aircraft. In addition, Dead-eye, as lead scout, was carrying special equipment for dealing with land-mines and booby-traps; wire-cutters and hessian for clearing barbed-wire entanglements; and an M23 grenade-launcher, which could be fixed to the barrel of his sniper rifle.

The march into the mountains was no less demanding than the rehearsal of the previous day. Even the lower, flatter slopes were filled with wadis, dried-up seasonal watercourses into which the men had to descend before climbing out again. The windswept plains were a treacherous combination of lava remains, soft sand and silt. Eventually leaving the lowlands behind, they were confronted by highlands of limestone, sandstone and igneous rocks.

Though not forced to endure the relentless heat

of day, they suffered its opposite: air so cold that they were breathing steam. Frost doubled the danger normally presented by loose stones and gravel. Dead-eye could see with great clarity through the eerie green glow of his PNGs, but the other men were dependent on the moonlight, which, reflecting off the ice and frost, rendered the darkness around these gleaming patches almost pitch-black. Nevertheless, they gradually adjusted to the darkness, and were soon on the level ground at the summit of the lowest of the series of ridges.

Not wanting the men to be silhouetted against the skyline, Dead-eye led them down the other side of the ridge, towards the deeper darkness far below. They would have to cross four ridges to get to their chosen OP, which was above an Arab village, and had to do it the hard way, by keeping out of sight. This meant marching up and down the sheer slopes instead of taking the path that circled around the ridges and joined them all. It would be a long, arduous march.

For many of the men, this hike from one peak to the other reminded them of 'cross-graining the bukets' in Malaya – marching from one summit to the next. The new men, on the other hand, were reminded of their hellish forced march across the Pen-y-Fan, the highest peak in the Brecon Beacons, at the culmination of Test Week during Selection Training. Known as the 'Fan Dance', it was probably the most demanding of all the tests undergone by SAS recruits – and this trek from one summit to another was certainly no easier.

But they kept at it, leaning forward as they ascended, slipping and sliding as they descended, whipped constantly by an icy wind and marching with great care in the deceptive moonlight. If they were soon feeling physically exhausted, they were also rendered psychologically so by the need for constant alertness as they strained to see by the moonlight, often mistaking shifting shadows and wind-blown foliage for the stealthy movements of enemy snipers. The relief, when they discovered their mistake, was often as brutal on their nervous systems as the fear that they were about to be shot at.

In fact, the only living creatures they saw on the mountains other than themselves were the odd ibex or oryx. Surprisingly, people did live here. In the valleys an occasional stone tower house or mud-brick hovel with stone foundations could be seen, usually standing alone, though some were in walled hamlets on the edge of meagre patches of cultivated land.

When such dwellings were seen, Dead-eye would give the patrol a rest while he entered details of the area in his logbook, including the exact location and size of the houses, hamlets or cultivated lands. Had any enemy troop movements been seen, he would have entered those as well.

Reaching their high ridge location before first light, the patrol divided into two groups, then constructed two temporary OPs spaced well apart and overlooking an Arab hamlet in the valley below. The OPs were of the star formation, with four 'legs' shaped like a cross: one for the sentry, one for the observer, and the other two serving as rest bays in which the men lay on their waterproof ponchos. To prevent the OPs being observed from the air, they were covered with camouflage netting strewn with stones, dust and any scrap of foliage to be found on the surrounding ground. By dawn, when the OPs were finished, the men designated as observers were doing just that with the aid of binoculars, while the others ate a breakfast of biscuits, chocolate and cold water. No fires could be lit because the smoke would have given away their position, so they continued to freeze.

In fact, the climb had taken so long, in such bitterly cold conditions, that the men had forgotten just how hot it could be during the day. They found out within the hour, when the sun melted the frost on the rocks, the flies and mosquitoes returned in force, and a heat haze shimmered up from the ground. By mid-morning the sun was fierce; by noon it was close to unbearable and made worse for the men because of the need to remain cooped up under the low-hanging camouflage netting.

The hamlet they were observing was believed to be a centre for Yemeni guerrillas, though none were seen throughout that long day. A few Arab men went out to till the small, sparse field, veiled women washed clothes around what looked like a desert spring, and children ran about between barking dogs and animals. None of the men looked remotely like guerrillas and no weapons were to be seen anywhere.

By late afternoon, it was clear to Dead-eye that if guerrillas had ever been in the hamlet, they were long gone by now. He entered this observation in his logbook, then turned to Ken and whispered: 'We're only supposed to spend one day here, which is just as well. There's nothing down there. We'll break up the OPs and move out under cover of darkness.'

'I can't wait,' the corporal replied without a trace of irony.

The rest of the day passed slowly, forcing the men to draw on the patience they had learnt back at Hereford. While none of them lost their concentration completely – they had been trained too rigorously for that – each had his own way of distracting himself from the tedium.

Dead-eye and Jimbo, the two most experienced men in the patrol, had the most concentration and needed little distraction other than repeatedly going over in their minds every detail of the patrol: whose turn it was for sentry duty or rest; every detail of the landscape and any sign of movement on it; any visible activity in the settlement below; the position of the sun in its sinking and the exact time of last light. Jimbo watched and listened while Dead-eye scribbled periodically in his logbook.

The young signaller, Derek Dickerson, was kept busy constantly monitoring the various wavebands on his radio and sending encoded messages from Dead-eye back to the base camp. However, while not thus engaged, his mind tended to wander to thoughts of his old mates back in 264 Signals

Squadron, Royal Corps of Signals, as well as to various girlfriends.

Also easily distracted by vivid memories of his love life was the patrol's medical specialist, Lance-Corporal Larry Johnson, formerly of the Royal Army Medical Corps (RAMC) and the same age as Dickerson. Larry was particularly distracted by thoughts of his latest and most serious girlfriend, Cathy Atkinson, a nineteen-year-old bank clerk whom he had met through a group of friends at a pub in his home town of Paignton.

If Larry was lying belly down in the OP's sentry leg he was fully concentrating, but the minute he had nothing to do he would find himself silently singing pop songs while aching with longing for Cathy. He choked up, in particular, at recalling Roy Orbison's *It's Over*, even though his affair with Cathy had hardly begun. Convinced that he was in love with her and could not live without her, Larry was nevertheless angered by the way in which she could repeatedly impinge on his thoughts, even when he was trying so hard to concentrate. It did not seem like a manly affliction and caused him to doubt himself.

Lance-Corporal Les Moody, on the other hand, was experienced enough to let his mind wander when tedium threatened yet regain full concentration when it was called for. Also keen on pop music, his head was presently filled with *A Hard Day's Night*, which had a certain aptness under these conditions. Indeed, as Les well knew, the only reason this war in Aden was not being reported by the British press was that Fleet Street was presently obsessed with the Beatles, virtually to the exclusion of all else.

Though only twenty-five, Les looked a lot older than the other lance-corporals, mainly because of his badly scarred left eye, broken nose and slightly twisted lower lip, all of which had been gained in various fist-fights in the pubs of Southend. Formerly of the 3rd Battalion, Royal Green Jackets, Les had served in Malaya and Borneo. Between those engagements he had married a local girl, Alison, on impulse – she had practically begged him, he liked to think – and fathered two sons. Though he treated his family decently during his few visits home, he had little interest in domesticity and preferred to be doing a man's work with the Regiment. He thought of Alison and the boys occasionally, but mostly dwelt on his occasional flings with other women, his days at the races – he was an inveterate gambler – various riotous evenings with his mates, and the tragedies and triumphs of his two previous campaigns with the SAS.

Les's good friend, Corporal Ken Brooke, when not on sentry duty, observing the Arab hamlet and the surrounding terrain with the keen eye of the thorough professional, would let his thoughts roam over a fairly wide spectrum. His thoughts roamed from his wife, of whom he was very fond, his three children – two girls and a boy – whom he adored, to the many interests he needed to keep himself busy, being a man of rich imagination and too much energy. Born and raised in Minehead, Ken was a keen wildlife photographer who, when on leave, spent many hours in Somerset's Brendon Hills and the Exmoor National Park, photographing ponies, wild red deer, foxes, rabbits and badgers. He also enjoyed fishing, hiking, train-spotting and collecting stamps, all of which he thought about while keeping alert for possible enemy movements on the landscape or unusual activities in the hamlet below. Though less bored than the others, he was nevertheless glad to see the sun go down, signalling as it did that it would soon be time to leave.

When darkness came, bringing with it the cold,

Dead-eye passed the word along to the other men that the OPs were to be carefully dismantled and all traces of them removed. When this had been done, in complete silence, he used hand signals to lead them away from the ridge, back down the way they had come, into a forbidding, rocky valley of moonlit darkness. They were temporarily protected from the wind there, but once they began climbing the opposite slope, it struck them with unexpected force, at once freezing them and almost bowling them over. Some of them were now grateful for the ruthless training they had undergone on the Brecon Beacons, realizing that without it they would not have survived this particular exercise.

Four hours later, when they were nearing the Dhala Road, dizzy with the cold and exhaustion, they were shocked to hear the sound of rifle fire and feel bullets zipping past their heads.

Marching in a diamond formation, they were able to drop to the ground and return the fire with a sustained fusillade from their personal weapons. Up ahead, they could see the spitting flames of the enemy rifles, which fortunately were not supported by machine-guns. Bullets stitched the earth around them and ricocheted off boulders. The shadowy figures of men ran back and forth up at the front, some gesticulating and shouting.

Out ahead, on point, but now belly down on the ground and about to fire his bolt-action sniper rifle, Dead-eye stopped himself just in time when he heard what he thought was English being shouted by the shadowy figures. Startled, he lowered his weapon, listened more carefully, and realized that he and his men were engaged in a fire-fight with soldiers of the British Army.

Raising his right hand, he indicated that the men behind him should stop firing, which they did only gradually, those at the back not being able to see him. When the hostile fire also tapered off tentatively, Dead-eye bawled: 'We're English! Stop firing! SAS!'

'Oh, Christ!' someone called out from the other side.

'D Squadron, 22 SAS!' Dead-eye called out. 'Sergeant Richard Parker!'

'Sergeant Shaun Clarke, Irish Guards. Stop firing, you men!'

As the last of the 'enemy' gunshots tapered off, Sergeant Clarke, his face blackened with 'cam' cream, stood up, shaking his head in disbelief and grinning ruefully. While their respective men also clambered sheepishly to their feet, wiping frost off their uniforms, Dead-eye and Clarke approached one another like guilty schoolboys. Even Dead-eye, normally impassive, was looking very self-conscious.

'Well,' he said, stopping in front of Sergeant Clarke, 'that was a close one.'

'*Very* close!' the other man replied, grinning. 'Sorry about that, but we weren't told there were friendly forces in the hills. We're just out on a proving patrol.'

'So are we – and *we* weren't told there were friendly forces in the area.'

'Lack of communication,' Clarke said. 'A right bloody cock-up. Anyone hurt?'

'No.'

'Good.' Clarke practically sighed with relief, then nodded down the ridge that led into a pool of deeper darkness. 'Are you heading back now?'

'Yes. Our RV's down there.'

'Lucky you. We've just started. But this little confrontation should give my boys something to think about. Keep them on their toes.' He grinned again and held out his hand. 'Well, best wishes, Sergeant.'

Dead-eye grinned as well, shaking Clarke's hand.

'Same to you,' he said, then marched back to his men, most of whom were grinning broadly at him. 'You men find this amusing?' he asked them. When they grinned even more broadly, he said firmly: 'Well, it's not. We almost shot up our own men and that's no laughing matter. We came out on a proving patrol, we're bringing back nothing, and now we've got to report a potentially fatal encounter with our own men. This patrol has been a bloody disaster, so wipe those grins off your faces.'

The men glanced uneasily at one another before adjusting their webbing, checking their weapons, and starting the rest of the march to the rendez-vous point, where they found the Saladins and Bedfords still grouped in a laager. Gratefully, the men loaded their weapons and other kit into the lorries, climbed in themselves, and settled down for the two-hour drive back to base. They all felt a bit foolish.

5

'Actually, it wasn't that bad,' Lieutenant-Colonel Callaghan said reassuringly to Dead-eye and Jimbo in the HQ tent at Thumier. 'Apart from almost being shot up by the Irish Guards – and they fired first, after all! – your patrol did all it was asked to do. I blame the shoot-out on a lack of communication between us and the greens. This time it was the fault of we Ruperts, so you've no need to worry.'

By 'greens' he meant the green-uniformed regular Army, while the word 'Ruperts' was normally used mockingly by the other ranks of the SAS to describe their own officers. In this case, the CO was using the terms as a means of light-heartedly taking the blame for the fire-fight with the Irish Guards. Dead-eye, who had always admired Callaghan, respected him even more for this.

They were facing each other across Callaghan's cluttered desk, which was actually a trestle table. The many papers and maps on the table were pinned down with stones to keep them from blowing away in the hot wind that gusted in from outside. At just after noon, the air in the tent was stifling and made all of them sweat.

'So when do we go back to the Radfan for some real work?' Dead-eye asked him.

Callaghan smiled and held his hand up like a traffic cop. 'Hold on there, Dead-eye. It *is* true that we intend mounting a major operation against the rebels in the Radfan, but we can't do it just yet.'

'Why?' Jimbo asked.

'According to the green slime,' Callaghan replied, referring to the Intelligence Corps, 'a couple of Yemeni-trained agents are perverting our intelligence and have to be dealt with before we can move again. Apparently these agents, who we thought were working for British Intelligence in Aden, are actually double agents, alternately giving us false information and passing on to the enemy information about our activities in the area. Either way, their treachery has led to many failed missions and casualties. So before we go back to the Radfan, we have to get rid of those men.'

'Why us?' Dead-eye asked. 'That's the job of the men based in Aden.'

'Normally, yes, but the way these double agents are operating indicates that they have many friends in our intelligence community. Should their activities be terminated by Intelligence hit men, or one of our Keeni-Meeni teams, the identity of those who do the job will almost certainly be revealed, endangering future operations by that unit. It is therefore felt that outsiders not known to that community should do it.'

'So if we're killed,' Jimbo said tartly, 'we can't be identified. If, on the other hand, we're captured and tortured into revealing our identity, the job still can't be traced back to the greens operating daily out of Aden.'

'Precisely,' Callaghan said.

Jimbo and Dead-eye glanced at one another, raising their eyebrows.

'Very nice for the greens,' Jimbo said, turning back to Callaghan. 'Not so nice for us, boss.'

Callaghan simply sighed and spread his hands in the air. 'What can I say? So do you want it or not?'

'What exactly is it?' Dead-eye asked. 'We've heard about the Keeni-Meeni teams in Aden. Is that what we'll be?'

'Temporarily,' the CO said. 'You'll be shown how to dress and act like an Arab, trained in the special 'double tap', then sent into the highly dangerous Crater and Sheikh Othman districts to do the job without backup or identification in the event of failure. Naturally it's a volunteer job.'

'Naturally,' Dead-eye replied sardonically.

'Yes or no?'

'Yes,' Dead-eye and Jimbo replied as one.

Callaghan smiled and placed his hands back on the table. 'Good. I knew you'd say that. Now go pack your kit, then meet me at the landing pad. We'll be lifted out on the Whirlwind and be away for two days.'

'Sounds good,' Dead-eye said. He and Jimbo pushed back their chairs and left the tent, stepping into the furnace of the midday heat. The sunlight temporarily dazzled them, making them blink and squint as they crossed the clearing between the HQ tent and the smaller tents being used as bashas. When they had adjusted to the searing brightness, they saw that the 25-pounders, 3-inch mortars and Browning 0.5-inch machine-guns in the hedgehogs spread out along the camp's perimeter were silhouetted starkly against the white haze of the sky and appeared unreal in the shimmering heat.

As usual, a lot of men, some from A Squadron, some from D, were lining up at the large mess tent, waiting to be served lunch, many of them wearing only shorts, socks and desert boots, all of them holding their tin plate, mug and eating utensils. As Dead-eye and Jimbo reached the tent they shared with Larry, a Wessex Mark 1 was landing beside the parked Whirlwind, covering the latter in a whipping cloud of sand and dust that also temporarily obscured the sun-scorched mountains beyond. That cloud even reached Dead-eye and Jimbo, making them both cough and cover their mouths as they ducked low and entered their tent. Larry was squatting on the rubber poncho stretched out beside his camp-bed, reading a copy of *Playboy*. He lowered it and glanced up when they entered.

'Filth,' Jimbo said with a straight face, keeping his head low to avoid scraping the top of the tent as he moved to his own side of it.

'What's that, Sarge? Filth? A bit of arse and tit never hurt anyone, Sarge. And it *does* give me something to think about.'

'You should be thinking of your nice girlfriend, Cathy,' Jimbo said, 'instead of wanking over that filthy rag.'

'I swear I haven't laid a hand on myself, Sarge,' Larry said, grinning without embarrassment. 'What's more, I only buy this so-called filthy rag for Hugh Hefner's profound articles on the *Playboy* philosophy – about sex, morality, hypocrisy and the need to be free. Really deep stuff, it is.'

'Yeah, so I've heard. He writes it when he's getting inspiration on his big round bed with birds all around him. A deep thinker that one – or deep diver, more like.'

'I'm taking everything,' Dead-eye said to Jimbo as he carefully packed his kit into his bergen. 'I'm leaving nothing behind for this lot of thieves. You should do the same.'

Dead-eye never discussed things like sex. Ever since he and his wife had divorced, he had kept to himself, having the odd affair, but not really becoming involved. Dead-eye did not like revealing his emotions and sex could make you do that. For that reason, it was best to treat it as a purely physical necessity. Life was easier that way.

'I will,' Jimbo replied, also packing his kit

into his bergen carefully so that all of it would fit. 'Lieutenant-Colonel Callaghan must have a trusting nature, but you and I know better.'

'Are you suggesting I'd steal your kit?' Larry asked, looking outraged.

'Not you,' Jimbo said. 'You wouldn't steal it because you're *in* here. But those other bastards' – he nodded towards the tent flaps, indicating the other SAS tents outside – 'would think we're a right pair of ponces if we left any kit behind. Then they'd nick it on principle.'

'You think so?'

Jimbo grinned and shook his head. 'Nah,' he said. 'Not really. It's just bad luck to leave your kit behind. All right, Dead-eye, I'm ready.'

'Where are you off to, then?' Larry asked.

'On a little trip,' Dead-eye replied. 'We'll be away for a couple of days, so you can have all this space to yourself.'

'To study philosophy,' Jimbo added ironically. 'See you soon, kid.'

They ducked even lower to leave the tent. Straightening up outside, they headed across the clearing, passing a sandbagged gun emplacement, to reach the helicopter LZ just beyond the perimeter. The Wessex had landed and was being unloaded by troops stripped to the waist and gleaming with sweat. Callaghan was standing under the slowly revolving props of the smaller Sikorski, holding his beret on his head as he gave covering instructions for his absence to Captain Ellsworth. He finished talking just as Dead-eye and Jimbo reached the chopper.

'Ah, good,' he said. 'You're here already. Clamber aboard, men.' Hauling up their bergens, Dead-eye and Jimbo climbed up into the Sikorski. They were strapping themselves into their seats, placing their bergens between their legs, when Callaghan followed them in and was in turn followed by the RAF crewman. The latter closed the door behind them, then bawled to the pilot that they were ready for take-off. Within seconds, the engines were roaring and the props were rotating at full speed, surrounding the chopper with a whirlwind of sand that it left behind only when it lifted up well above the earth. Glancing down as the chopper ascended, the three SAS men saw the collection of tents and circle of defensive hedgehogs shrinking until they had merged with the surrounding landscape of lava and desert, finally disappearing completely into it.

Only when the Whirlwind had stopped climbing and was flying horizontally above the parched mountain peaks was Callaghan able to make himself heard at all above the now reduced noise of the engines. Even so, he was forced to shout the whole time, and finally he said he would tell them what they needed to know when they were back on the ground.

They landed shortly afterwards at the RAF airfield at Aden. From there they were driven in a British Army 4×4 Willys jeep, which carried them along a dusty road to the military complex at Khormaksar, where the SAS Keeni-Meeni men were located. Sitting in the front of the jeep and now able to speak without shouting, Callaghan twisted around to face his two sergeants and explain what 'Keeni-Meeni' meant.

'The kind of clandestine plain-clothes operations we're mounting here originated with Major Frank Kitson during Kenya's Mau Mau campaign, which the SAS was briefly involved in. This led to the formation of a few so-called 'counter gangs', or anti-terrorist teams, composed of former terrorists and loyal tribesmen led by British officers disguised as natives. The same type of operation was also used in Cyprus as the basis of the undercover "Q" units.

'However, when we first set up a Close Quarters

Battle course here for a carefully selected group of SAS troopers, we knew that there was no hope of 'turning round' Arab terrorists and so decided to function more like the "Q" squads of the Palestine police as started by Roy Farran, a veteran of the wartime SAS who used a lot of his old buddies from that period. In some instances this involves driving around in Q cars, or unmarked cars, searching out possible Yemeni agents. In others, it involves picking up terrorists alive and bringing them in for questioning. But often it simply means shooting them before they manage to shoot you, which is exactly what they'll do if they recognize you. It's a highly dangerous, face-to-face business that requires lots of nerve.'

'So the basic idea,' Dead-eye said, taking lots of nerve for granted, 'is for disguised, plain-clothes SAS men to go into the alleyways and *souks* of Aden for undercover surveillance and the odd assassination.'

'An ugly word, Dead-eye, but I think you've got the message.'

'Keeni-Meeni's not such an ugly word. What does it mean?'

'It comes from a Swahili phrase that describes the movement of a snake in the long grass: sinuous and unseen. The same term later became a synonym in Africa – and with the slave trade in the Arabian Gulf – for undercover work. The British army picked it up during the Mau Mau campaign, and from Kenya it travelled to the SAS, here in Aden. We, however, relate it specifically to operations involving a standard operating procedure known as the double tap, which is what you're going to learn in one day as part of your quick CQB course in Khormaksar . . . Talking of which . . .'

Callaghan indicated straight ahead with a nod of his head as the jeep approached the heavily guarded military complex. After being checked thoroughly by the sentries at the gate, which had heavily armed sangars on either side, they were driven straight to Ballycastle House, a block of flats formerly used as married quarters but now the operational centre for the twenty-odd members of the SAS Keeni-Meeni squad. Once inside, they were introduced to Sergeant-Major Monnery, who was with the Long Range Desert Group during World War Two and was a founder member of the SAS, a 'green slime' SNCO, and now the man in charge of the Keeni-Meeni teams in Aden.

'As time is of the essence I'll now take my leave,' Callaghan said. 'Sergeant-Major Monnery will show you the ropes and return you to me when, and if, you succeed. Good luck, men.'

When the CO had left, Jimbo said: 'Well, well! If it isn't Wild Bill Monnery of the LRDG. And looking twenty years younger instead of twenty years older. Remember me, Sergeant-Major?'

'How could I forget you?' Monnery replied. 'Came crawling out of the African desert on your hands and knees, bloodied, blistered, black and blue, but with a grin on your stupid face.' He was referring to the extraordinary trek across the North African desert which Jimbo had made with other SAS men, including the legendary Captain John 'Jock' Lewes, creator of the Lewes bomb, after the raid against the Axis airfield at Nofilia in December 1941. As the LRDG sergeant in charge of the transport at the RV, 'Wild Bill' Monnery had been there to witness the extraordinary sight of the sun-scorched, tattered SAS men, having lost their transport, walking, stumbling and, as in Jimbo's case, crawling on hands and knees back to the RV after days in the desert. Now he grinned and put out his beefy hand to let Jimbo shake it. 'Nice to see you, Jimbo.'

'Nice to see *you*, Wild Bill.'

'Sergeant-Major Monnery to you,' Wild Bill

replied with mock outrage, withdrawing his hand and wiping it delicately on his shorts. 'Ah, well, here we go again.' He grinned at the impassive Dead-eye. 'And you're . . .?'

'Sergeant Richard Parker.'

'Known as Dead-eye,' Jimbo said.

'Ah, yes!' Wild Bill said softly, in admiration. 'I've heard all about you. The Telok Anson swamp and . . .'

'That's right,' Dead-eye interjected curtly. 'So what happens now?'

Experienced enough to know that there were barriers you did not cross, Wild Bill just nodded, then said, 'All right, men, come with me. I'll explain what we're up to on the way to the indoor firing range. But first you'll have to be kitted out with an Arab *futah*, which is what you'll be wearing when you go out on your mission.' He led them straight to a store room where a British Army private gave each of them an Arab robe, which they were told to put on immediately. This they did with considerable amusement, studying one another with wide grins when they had slipped their *futahs* over their heads and let them hang down around their body.

'We still don't look like Arabs,' Dead-eye said.

'You will when the times comes,' Wild Bill said. 'Now let's get to the firing range.'

'What we're doing here,' he told them as he led them along another corridor past the doors of the former married quarters, 'is exploiting the trick we developed in Palestine: namely, to disguise ourselves as locals, blend in with the local scenery and way of life, and seize on our targets as the opportunity arises. The high-risk areas of Crater and Sheikh Othman are like rabbit warrens, a maze of narrow alleys jam-packed with shops, stalls, Arabs and animals. You move there hemmed in on all sides, close up, practically nose to nose with your targets. For this reason, when we look for suitable SAS candidates for the Keeni-Meeni squads, we pick men who most resemble Arabs, with the hooked nose and prominent cheekbones of the Semite.'

'My nose is classically beautiful,' Jimbo said. 'I'm obviously in the wrong place.'

'We had to make an exception with you two,' Wild Bill said, 'because of the urgency of this situation. You were chosen not for your looks but because you've proven yourselves expert with the handgun and are known to be daring.'

'That's us!' Jimbo chirped.

'However, while you already know how to fire your 9-milli,' Monnery continued, referring to the Browning High Power handgun, 'what we're going to teach you is the double tap, which is the ability to very quickly draw the Browning from the folds of that *futah* you're wearing and fire it with perfect accuracy at close range.'

He led them through another door, into a large gymnasium converted into a combined firing range and CQB training area. It was, they noticed immediately, filled with Fijian SAS men, including a truly enormous soldier, well over six feet tall.

'Our Fijian brothers,' Wild Bill said. 'That black giant you're all staring at is Corporal Labalaba, the best Keeni-Meeni man we've got. Naturally his kind blends in with the scenery like you never could.' Wild Bill grinned broadly. 'You have to be careful of men like Labalaba. Not so long ago the Royal Anglian Regiment's Special Branch made the mistake of putting some men into the Sheikh Othman district without telling us. Armed and dressed as Arabs, they were mistaken for terrorists by Labalaba's plain-clothes patrol and shot to hell in a few seconds. Labalaba doesn't stop to ask questions, so watch out.' Turning towards a dark-haired, grinning SAS corporal who had just approached them, swathed in a *futah*, he said: 'And this is . . .'

'Trooper Terry Malkin!' Dead-eye explained, giving a rare grin. 'I forgot you'd be posted here, Terry.'

'Three months in the rabbit warrens of Aden,' Terry replied. 'It beats rotting at home.'

The two men shook hands.

'In the three months he's been here,' Wild Bill told them, 'Trooper Malkin's become one of our best Keeni-Meeni operators. Unfortunately for us, three months is the limit for anyone engaged in this work, so after he joins you in this operation, he'll be rejoining the Regiment – going back with you, in fact. In the meantime, he'll teach you all you need to know and take you out on that patrol. Since he's not going to be here tomorrow, it won't matter if he's identified in the *souks*.'

'Terry's going to teach *me* to shoot?' Dead-eye asked, already looking offended.

'Not to shoot,' Wild Bill replied. 'To double tap while wearing that Arab gear, which is something quite different. Now you take note, Dead-eye.' Grinning, Wild Bill took a seat in a hard wooden chair nearby and lit up a cigarette, letting Terry take over.

Instead of having them get used to the firing range, Terry first demonstrated the double tap.

'This SOP was devised by Major Roy Farran during World War Two,' he explained, 'but Farran taught his men what was then this rather unorthodox triangular firing posture . . .' – Terry demonstrated the stance – 'known as the "Grant-Taylor Method". He also insisted that his men should be able to put six rounds through a playing-card at 15 yards.'

Suddenly, with startling speed, Terry spun to the side, whipped a Browning 9mm High Power handgun out from under his robes, spread his legs, raised the pistol two-handed in the triangular firing posture and fired off six shots in quick succession at the target at the end of the firing alley. Only when he had finished firing did the half-deafened men see that his target had been an Ace of Hearts suspended where a proper target would normally have been. A large jagged hole indicated that practically all six shots had gone through the centre of the card.

Terry turned back to face them. 'We expect the same of you,' he said, reloading his pistol. 'You have until tomorrow.'

'Christ!' Jimbo whispered, staring in disbelief at the card.

'Let's get started, gentlemen,' Wild Bill said, exhaling a cloud of cigarette smoke. 'We haven't got all day.'

'Yes, we have,' Terry replied.

They did indeed have all day and Terry ensured that it was a long one, taking them repeatedly through the double tap. Both Dead-eye and Jimbo were experts with the handgun, but the trick in this instance was withdrawing it from beneath the long *futah* and bringing it into the firing position quickly enough, and accurately enough, to cut down the enemy before he could react. As this was made no easier by the complicated folds of the robe, they had to rehearse the withdrawal for hours before getting as far as the actual firing range.

While taking their training seriously, both sergeants could not help being amused at the idea of being trained by a trooper who normally took orders from them. This led to many jokes, which Terry took in good part.

Eventually, however, both men had mastered the rapid withdrawal technique and were able to go on to the firing range, where it was combined with shooting. In this part of the training both men came into their own, showing that their extensive experience of armed combat in many previous operations had honed their shooting skills to a fine edge. Before the long day had ended both were withdrawing the handgun, bringing it into the firing position, and firing with absolute accuracy, repeatedly piercing the playing card right through its centre. When they had done this at least a dozen times, with no misses, Terry, having enjoyed his brief moment of authority, called it a day.

'You blokes are as good as me now,' he said, puffed up with pride. 'We'll go into Aden tomorrow. For now, let's have dinner.'

'Yes, boss,' said Dead-eye and Jimbo simultaneously, before both burst out laughing.

6

Awakening at first light the following morning, Dead-eye, Jimbo and Terry had a shower and shave, then dressed in their olive-green gear, or OGs, and went to the NAAFI canteen in Ballycastle House for a breakfast of fried eggs, bacon, sausage, baked beans and toast, washed down with a couple of mugs each of steaming hot tea.

'Better than that noggie food, I can tell you,' Jimbo said with relish, scooping up his fried egg on his fork.

'That's not very nice, Sarge,' Terry said with some feeling. 'They're Arabs, not noggies.'

'They're all brownies to me,' Jimbo said. 'Apart from that, I've nothing against 'em. I just don't like their grub.'

'If you like your scran so much,' Dead-eye said,

'why don't you fill your mouth with it and let us have some peace?'

'Good old Dead-eye,' Jimbo snorted, shoving a piece of sausage into his mouth and winking at Terry. 'Always sticking up for the lower orders. He developed his little fondness for our coloured brothers in Malaya and Borneo.'

'An enemy to respect,' Dead-eye said. 'You had to admire them.'

'I don't respect anyone trying to nail me. I just treat 'em with care. Your respect for blokes trying to kill you has always bleedin' amazed me.'

'If he respects men who are trying to kill him,' Terry said with a cheeky grin, 'he'll be full of respect in the *souks* of Aden. Have my NCOs finished their breakfast? Good! Let's take off.'

'Is that an order or a request?' Jimbo asked, letting the cocky young trooper know who was in charge.

'We're running late.'

'There's your answer,' Dead-eye said.

Jimbo grinned, greatly amused by the confidence Terry had picked up since joining the Keeni-Meeni squads. 'I'm pretty sure we're in good hands,' he said.

'Thanks a lot, Sarge,' said Terry.

They returned to the 'spider', their sleeping quarters, where they set about making themselves look like Arabs by darkening their skin with a mixture of coffee, lamp-black, iodine and potassium permanganate. Some of them, including Dead-eye, had done the same in Malaya when passing themselves off as Malays or Chinese. The basic mixture could be lightened or darkened with ease, which made it highly adaptable for a wide variety of skin tones. In this case, when the three men had created a colouring similar to that of the local Arabs, they applied it carefully to their faces, hands, wrists and all the way up their arms, to ensure that no white skin would be glimpsed should the loose sleeves of the *futah* ride up. As they were wearing Arab sandals, instead of shoes, they also dyed their feet, ankles and legs up to the knees. Finally, even though they would be wearing the Arab *shemagh* on their heads, they dyed their hair black to ensure that their alien hair colour would not be betrayed by loose strands.

'This is the bit I love most of all,' Terry said, examining himself carefully in the full-length mirror. 'Dressing up for the part. It brings out the natural actor in me. Changes my personality completely. Don't you think so, Sarge?'

'You don't have a personality,' Jimbo replied. 'You're just a walking vacuum in a uniform. Without that, you'd be nothing.'

'Not a uniform today, Sarge. I'm an Arab now.'

'Fucking Lawrence of Arabia, more like it,' Jimbo laughed. 'And every bit as barmy.'

'All these Arabs are mad,' Terry said. Now let's go out and prove it.'

The joking, Dead-eye knew, was a means of holding in check the healthy tension that was now taking hold of them as they thought of mingling with the Arabs, practically face to face. For all the bullshit, the three of them knew, as they strapped their holstered Brownings in the cross-draw position under their *futahs*, that what they were about to do was very dangerous indeed and that they could easily end up dead – either shot by the enemy or murdered by an irate mob after being caught attempting the double tap. In particular, irrespective of the reassuring feel of the 9-milli in the holster strapped around his waist, Dead-eye felt unprotected without his L42A1 bolt-action sniper rifle and heavy bandoliers of 7.62mm rounds; in truth, he felt almost naked.

Walking to the motor pool with their faces

darkened and robes flapping in the breeze, they received a lot of derisory remarks from 'greens' and other SAS men. Used to this by now, Terry just grinned and gave the jokers the finger. At the motor pool, they had to sign for a 'Q' car, or unmarked car, this one a particularly battered old Beetle of the kind used by a lot of the local Arab traders. To emphasize its well-worn appearance, it had been packed with cardboard boxes, wrapping paper with Arabic lettering and other junk merchandise, such as cigarettes, cheap binoculars and cameras, and boxes of ballpens, as sold by the traders in the bum boats.

'Christ,' Jimbo said, studying the car. 'I don't mind it looking so bad, but it smells like it's been pissed in.'

'It probably has been, at one time or another,' Terry said. 'The piss of fear, Sergeant.'

Glancing sideways at Terry as they clambered into the messy, foul-smelling car, Dead-eye realized that the young trooper had matured tremendously since his hellish experiences in Borneo, only a year ago. Straight out of Hereford, Terry had been very unsure of himself at first, the constant butt of the other men's jokes, but he had soon proved to be an excellent soldier, particularly at the climax of the campaign when, with Corporals Alf Laughton (now a member of the directing staff at 22 SAS Training Wing, Hereford) and Pete Welsh, they had fought their way back to base through the hellish swamps surrounding the River Koemba. Welsh had died at the climax of that operation – shot off a walkway, to plunge to his death in the roaring torrents of a gorge over a hundred feet below. Terry, however, had not only survived it but, as the team's signaller, protected his all-important radio every inch of the way. Shaped into a toughened, experienced trooper by that frightful experience, he had been a natural choice for the present highly dangerous task. Now, he was more than a little confident, even with his NCOs.

As Terry drove the two sergeants out of the guarded gates of the military complex and along the dusty road to Aden, in the shadow of the volcanic mountains, he told them a little about the city.

'Being located at the southern entrance to the Red Sea,' he began rather pedantically, 'it's mainly been used as a commercial centre and refuelling stop for ships. However, it first really gained importance with the opening of the Suez canal in

1869, then with the development of the oilfields in Arabia and the Persian Gulf.' Jimbo rolled his eyes, but Terry did not notice. 'It has a few small industries, such as light manufacturing, evaporation of sea water to obtain marine salt, and boatbuilding. Naturally, as a free port, it's much loved by tourists and other seaborne travellers, despite the presence of the armed greens in the streets.'

'Nothing like a little duty free,' Jimbo said, grinning at Dead-eye, 'to make the tourists lose their common sense. So give us the *layout*, lad.'

'Ah!' Terry exclaimed, catching the older man's drift. 'It consists of three sections: Crater, the old commercial quarter; at-Tawahi, the business section; and Ma'alah, the native harbour area. We do most of our work in Crater or around the harbour area.'

'With the tourists,' Dead-eye said.

'Right, Sarge. And those tourists are a bit of a problem when it comes to making a hit.'

'Block your line of fire, do they?' Jimbo asked.

'Exactly. Or go into a panic when you're trying to make your getaway. Run right across your path of flight. Either that or the Arabs, when they see the dead man, take it out on the nearest white person. And who's that?'

'Someone off a boat,' Dead-eye said.

'Exactly,' Terry said. 'Tourists!'

Arriving at the harbour area, they drove through narrow, crowded streets, past the many duty-free shops and food stalls, and parked on Tawahi Main Road, close to the fenced-off harbour, but a good distance from the armed British soldiers guarding the gateway to the Aden Port Trust. The P & O liner *Himalaya* was anchored in the bay, looming large beyond the iron railings, concrete municipal buildings and warehouses of the docks, but passengers were coming ashore from the transit craft and emerging from the gateway to stare goggle-eyed, first at the brazenly importuning taxi drivers, then at the packed, dusty streets of the town.

'Ships' passengers are often a bit frightened when they first set eyes on this area,' Terry said, indicating Tawahi Main Road and its many shops, smoking and steaming food stalls, Sunni and Saydi Muslims, Hindus, Yemeni Jews, holy men and traders, beggars and thieves, veiled women and dirty children – all watched by stony-faced armed British troops – the 'greens' – armed with Sten guns and self-loading rifles. 'But the only real danger here is in having your pocket picked or losing your money when you buy a phoney Parker pen or a pair of binoculars without lenses. The real danger is up in Crater, where most of the terrorists hang around.'

'So what are we doing here?' Dead-eye asked him.

'Just filling you in, Sarge.'

Starting the car again, Terry drove at a crawl along the busy road, into the seething heart of Aden, where the Arabs were as dense as flies and every bit as noisy. As the car passed through side streets filled with shops, all run by Arabs though most had British names such as the London Store or the New Era, Dead-eye took note of the shopkeepers sitting outside on wooden chairs, the tourists haggling as they sipped tea, the tense soldiers standing guard at nearly every corner, and realized that this place, no matter what Terry thought, was a powder-keg waiting to be lit.

'Take the 9-milli out here and fire it,' he said, 'and you'd have bloody chaos.'

'Too right,' Terry confirmed. 'The tourists would shit themselves, the Arabs would take it out on the tourists, and the greens would open fire on the Arabs. A right bloody mess, all right.'

'And Crater?'

'No greens. Few tourists. Just the Arab — ours

and theirs. The ones on our side are poor and can't take sides, so we're all on our own up there.'

'You like it, don't you?' Dead-eye said.

'Yes, I do,' Terry confessed.

'Danger can be addictive,' Jimbo said. 'You've got the bug, kid.' He glanced up the lower slopes of the mountain beyond the town and saw a triangular-shaped maze of white, flat-roofed buildings, partly covered by a layer of dense, low cloud. 'Is that Crater up there?'

'Yes. That's where we're going. We'll be there in ten minutes.' Turning another street corner, Terry left the shops behind, then turned again almost immediately, passing a wire fence that ran alongside the road skirting the lower slopes of the mountains. 'Here,' he said, reaching into the glove compartment and withdrawing the photos of two male Arabs. 'These are the two we're after. They live down in Aden but visit Crater every afternoon to collect funds from various shopkeepers for their Yemeni brothers up in the Radfan. We'll just have to trawl the various places we know they go to and hope to catch them before the day's done. If we do, we finish them off with a double tap, then get the hell out of there.'

'Are we going in this car?' Dead-eye asked.

'No. We park in a residential street at the edge of Crater and walk into the commercial centre. When we've completed the job, we'll all make our own way back to the car, then skedaddle out of there.'

'How long does the first man at the car give the others to reach him?'

'He either gives them five minutes or takes off at the first sign of trouble — such as avenging Arabs.'

'But the other two could just be lost or captured,' Dead-eye said. 'Don't we go back to find out?'

'No. And we don't pick up the wounded or go back for anyone who gets lost. That's why we don't carry identification. It's a win-or-lose game.'

'Fucking great,' Jimbo said.

'Sensible,' Dead-eye corrected him.

'I agree,' Terry said. 'The Arabs are too volatile and unpredictable, so there's no turning back.'

While Terry drove towards Crater, Dead-eye and Jimbo studied the photos of the two Arabs more carefully. When they were sure they had taken in every feature of the two men and would recognize them if they saw them, they put a match to the pictures, let them burn up, then threw the blackened remains out of the car window, thus ensuring that no evidence of their intentions

111

would be found on their person if they were caught.

They reached Crater after a ten-minute drive along a road that wound up the lower slopes of the volcanic mountain. Terry's 'commercial centre' was actually a rabbit warren of narrow streets and *souks*, all packed with shops, small, enclosed bazaars, cafés, Arabs and animals. Many of the Arabs were playing draughts or other games at tables outside the cafés. Others were smoking opium pipes. Nearly all were drinking mint tea. The alleys and *souks* were filled with the smoke from burning braziers and steam from pots of cooking food or boiling tea. Men were leading cattle through the narrow, packed *souks*, letting them ease their way, mooing, through the tide of people, which included many children and their veiled mothers. There were few cripples or blind people, for most of them were down in the harbour area, exploiting the tourists. Even without them, there was still a fearful crush.

'You were right,' Dead-eye said, 'there's no room to breathe here.'

'Which means little room to manoeuvre,' Jimbo added. 'No wonder it calls for special training.'

Terry grinned, pleased. 'Yes,' he said. 'The

training isn't just for accuracy with the 9-milli; it's to get up your speed. When you see the target, you don't have too much time to prepare yourself and take aim. You have to make an instant calculation even as you're whipping out the gun. You have to shoot and scoot, so make sure you get it right the first time. There are no second chances.'

After driving around as much of the area as was possible given the narrowness of the *souks*, pointing out as they went the gathering places for enemy agents, Terry parked on the southern edge of the densely populated area, in a street of flat-roofed stone houses that contained few people and ran out to the mountain slopes, thus providing a quick escape route. After automatically checking that their Brownings were in the proper, cross-draw position under their robes and that their make-up was still in good shape, the men got out of the car, surprised by how hot the sun was, even though it was still overcast.

'It's always like this,' Terry explained, glancing at the few Arabs, mostly women and children, wandering about the residential street. 'Bloody muggy. Are you all set?' Dead-eye and Jimbo both nodded. 'All right,' Terry continued. 'From this point on, we don't speak. We keep well apart

– we'll be less noticeable that way – but make sure we're always in sight of each other. If any Arab speaks to you, try to avoid replying, but without actually offending him. I usually just nod and keep walking. If that's not possible, reply in Arabic, but as briefly as possible, as if you're in a hurry. First man who sees the target pots him. If we all see him at once, we all shoot at once. Try to get as close as possible before firing. We run for it the minute we've fired – we can't stop to check that he's dead. Escape under cover of the confusion caused by the shooting. Any questions?'

Dead-eye and Jimbo both shook their heads.

'I'll lead the way, stopping at the various likely meeting places I've already shown you. You keep a good distance behind me. When I stop, you fan out around me, though still well away from me, mingling with the crowd. Let's go.'

By leading them along the relatively quiet residential street, Terry was able to give them time to adjust to the unease they felt when walking past real Arabs. Though their faces were dyed dark and *shemaghs* half-covered their faces, both Dead-eye and Jimbo felt as white as ever and could not accept that their disguise would pass muster this close to the women and children in the street. In the event, though many of the children and a few of the women and older men glanced at them, none of them seemed to notice anything unusual, and they reached the end of the street without incident.

But as they turned into a narrow, thronging *souk*, a veritable river of densely packed Arab traders and their clamouring customers, both men stiffened automatically, expecting to be detected instantly. Dead-eye was not the kind to admit to feeling fear, but even he could not stop a fleeting moment of panic as he followed Terry, a good ten yards ahead. They passed along the crowded *souk*, no more than an alleyway, between open shopfronts piled high with fruit, vegetables, nuts, carpets, pots and pans, and just about every kind of local household implement. Here, Dead-eye soon noticed, there was little sign of the cameras, binoculars, transistor radios, leather goods and pens that were so popular with the tourists down in the harbour area. Clearly this was a genuine Arab quarter, serving only local people.

Those Arabs were around him now, pressing in on all sides, practically breathing in his face, letting him smell their sweat. He lowered his head as much as possible while still glancing about him, taking in every detail of the narrow *souk*, which, he now noticed, had still narrower, starkly shadowed, but less crowded alleyways leading off it.

Even as Dead-eye was considering the side alleyways as possible escape routes, the *souk* opened out into a small, busy plaza full of cafés and food stalls. Now at the other side of the plaza, Terry stopped and indicated, with an almost imperceptible nod of his head, a café directly opposite where he was standing. There were tables and chairs outside, most of them occupied by Arabs reading newspapers, sipping mint tea or playing dominoes or chess.

Recalling that this was one of the meeting places of the guerrilla agents, Dead-eye also stopped walking and leaned against the nearest wall, as if watching the world go by. Glancing sideways, he saw Jimbo doing the same and was relieved that, at least from this distance, he really did blend in with the crowd.

After signalling, with another prearranged, subtle hand movement, that Dead-eye and Jimbo were to remain where they were, Terry approached the café, wove his way between the tables and disappeared inside. Watching the doorway, Dead-eye tensed himself for the sound of gunfire, but none came. Eventually Terry reappeared. He turned along the side of the café and entered another *souk*.

Dead-eye and Jimbo followed, still keeping well apart. This *souk* was just as narrow as the first one had been, but Dead-eye and Jimbo were starting to slip more naturally into their roles, gaining confidence from not being detected; now they found the experience less hair-raising and, in Jimbo's case, even fun. Dead-eye, as always, took a more pragmatic view, treating it purely as a job of work and determined to do it right.

Though frequently having to stop and press themselves against the wall to let Arab traders pass with heavily laden wheeled barrows, or to avoid cows being herded to market through the narrow *souk*, they eventually reached another busy square, its four sides packed with shops and cafés. Here, again, they kept well apart, each taking a separate side of the square, though all three of them faced the café which Terry had indicated with a barely perceptible nod of his head.

Clearly Terry had learned something about his quarry when he had entered the previous establishment, because this time he took a seat at one of the tables and ordered mint tea. While Terry had been specially trained in Arabic at the Hereford and Army School of Languages and was, reportedly, fairly fluent, Dead-eye felt that he was taking a greater chance than was necessary by sitting at a table and ordering mint tea from an Arab waiter. In any case, another Arab could strike up a conversation, which would make things very tricky.

Dead-eye was even more convinced that Terry was getting too cocky when, half an hour later, he ordered food from what looked like a roadside trader serving a cheap couscous from an unhygienic charcoal stove on wheels. Surprisingly, he got away with it, but watching him tuck into it, expertly scooping the steamed wheat grain up into his mouth like the other Arabs, Dead-eye felt a combination of admiration for Terry's new confidence and concern that it was becoming a dangerous display of bravado.

Glancing sideways, he saw that Jimbo was also intently watching Terry at his table, either simply envying him for having the opportunity to eat or, like Dead-eye, worried that he was playing with fire.

Another fifteen minutes passed. Terry finished his meal, crumpled the heavy paper it had been served in, threw it to the ground at his feet, as others had done, and sat back again, watching the world go by. Dead-eye and Jimbo, meanwhile, meandered around the square, not wanting to remain too long in one place in case an Arab spoke to them, but always needing to be close to the café that Terry was watching.

Dead-eye was only about five yards from the door when he saw Terry move. It happened so fast that even Dead-eye was almost taken by surprise. As a well-built Arab wearing a well-cut suit with a shirt and tie stepped out of the café, Terry pushed his chair back, stood up and walked forward as if about to enter. The Arab did not even bother to look up when Terry, still advancing, reached under the flowing *futah*. Only when Terry had whipped out his pistol, spread his legs and was taking aim, about to fire two-handed, did the man realize what was happening and try to duck sideways. He was too late.

Locking his arms and bending his legs slightly as he had been taught in the 'Killing House' in Hereford, aiming square at his target from a distance of less than five yards, holding the pistol firmly and applying pressure equally between the thumb and fingers of the firing hand, Terry fired two rounds in quick succession.

Dead-eye and Jimbo were still reaching for their weapons when the double roar of Terry's Browning deafened them and the quarry was violently punched back, blood spurting from his chest, to crash over the table directly behind him. The customers cried out and scattered as the table collapsed beneath the shot man and he hit the ground in a welter of smashing bottles and glasses that were spattered with his spurting blood.

Even as the Arab was flopping over onto his side, one bloody hand clawing feebly at the ground, another, also in European dress, emerged from the café, firing a pistol at Terry. The bullets missed and were whining into the scattering, bawling crowd as Dead-eye and Jimbo raised their own weapons in the two-handed firing position and simultaneously discharged two rounds at the man. Their combined double tap, plus Terry's, made the man drop his pistol, convulse wildly, slam back into the door frame and slide to the ground even as his assailants were turning away to flee.

Glancing back, Dead-eye saw a third man emerge from the café, turn in the opposite direction and race around the far corner of the building. Terry saw him too. Without a word, he turned back, vaulting over a table, above the panic-stricken

Arab customers lying on the ground, to run after the man who had fled. Realizing that the third man must be the second target, and that the second man killed was probably only a bodyguard, Dead-eye instantly followed Terry and was in turn followed by Jimbo, who bowled over a few of the Arabs in his haste to catch up with the other two.

As Dead-eye turned the corner of the café, an irate Arab bawled abuse and rushed at him, wielding a knife. Dead-eye ducked. The knife slashed through the air where his head had been. Dead-eye kneed the man in the groin, then clubbed him with the butt of his pistol as he doubled up, gasping.

Dead-eye raced ahead as the Arab was falling. He followed Terry along another narrow alleyway, hearing Jimbo's rapid footsteps echoing behind him. Luckily, this *souk* did not contain shops or stalls, which made progress easier, though the three of them bowled over strolling Arabs as they ran, causing startled or angry shouts to erupt in their wake.

The chase led them eventually to the other, even poorer side of Crater, to a rubbish-strewn square wreathed in smoke from the many open fires and food stalls scattered between the tables and chairs of the shabby cafés.

Clearly knowing where his quarry was heading, Terry had replaced his pistol under his *futah* and stopped running before reaching the square. Instead of entering the square, he took a seat on a wooden bench along the wall of the street leading into it. He then indicated with a nod of his head that Dead-eye and Jimbo should join him, which they did, one sitting either side of him, the three of them together taking up the whole of the bench to ensure that no real Arabs could join them. As no one was near them, they could talk in low voices.

'Our man's in a house between two smaller houses, just about visible from where I'm sitting,' Terry informed them. 'He can't see us from there, though I can see the house, and if we're patient and don't enter the square, he'll finally decide that we didn't follow him and come out again. If he does, I'll see him before he sees us. When I make my move, you back me up, keeping your eye out for anyone who makes a move towards me. If they do, finish them off.'

Terry glanced along the alleyway to check that no one was coming, then studied the busy square again. 'In the meantime,' he said with great authority, forgetting that he was with two NCOs, 'let's pretend we're three old friends, just sitting and talking. We can speak in English as long as no one is around. If Arabs pass, you stop speaking and I'll do all the talking in Arabic, keeping my voice low. That should do the trick.'

'I can't bloody believe this,' Jimbo whispered at the other side of Terry. 'We're both taking orders from this trooper. We're hanging on his every word.'

'He's done all this before,' Dead-eye replied, talking across Terry as if he was not there, though in a soft voice, 'and knows what he's doing. So let's give him his due.'

'Bloody amazing, is all I can say. Would you credit it?'

'Thanks, Sarge,' Terry said. 'I take that as a compliment.'

They talked softly for the next fifty minutes, sometimes trading the traditional SAS bullshit but just as often passing comments on the movements of the many Arabs in the narrow alleyway and the busier square. The fifty minutes became an hour, then two, and when another half-hour had passed without sight of their quarry, even Dead-eye, whose patience was legendary, was starting to feel restless. Suddenly, however, he felt Terry stiffening beside him and Jimbo, at the other side of Terry, asked: 'Is that him?'

Terry nodded and stood as casually as possible, slipping his hand under his *futah* as he did so. Dead-eye and Jimbo followed him as he walked into the square, picking up speed with each step, then suddenly breaking into a run. His quarry, another well-fed Arab in an expensive suit, saw him coming and actually straightened up, shocked.

Dead-eye and Jimbo were fanning out on either side of Terry, both withdrawing their pistols, when an unwitting taxi-driver braked to a halt just ahead of Terry.

The rear passenger door opened.

Terry was just coming abreast of the taxi when an Englishman started to get out. Without breaking his pace, Terry reached out with his left hand to push the Englishman back into the vehicle. The Englishman was straightening up and about to step out again when Terry reached under his *futah* and withdrew his Browning with a quick, smooth sweep of his right hand. Spreading his legs to steady himself, he aimed the pistol at the Arab who had just emerged from the mud-brick house straight ahead and was about to duck down between the pavement tables of the cafés on either side.

Terry fired six shots in rapid succession, punching the Arab backwards, almost lifting him off the ground and then bowling him into the dirt.

As the Arab fell, a woman screamed hysterically from inside the taxi, many Arabs in the square bawled warnings or shouted out in fear, and Terry turned back to be faced with the shocked tourist, half in and half out of the taxi.

'Sorry about that,' Terry said to the Englishman, then pushed him back into the taxi, slammed the door shut, and was disappearing into the crowd as the Muslim taxi-driver, more familiar with the area than his passenger, noisily ground his gears, made a sharp U-turn, and roared off the way he had come, the dust churned up by his spinning wheels settling over the dead Arab on the ground.

Not having fired a shot, but now holding their pistols, Dead-eye and Jimbo raced after the fleeing Terry, giving him cover until he had disappeared into the nearest *souk*. One foolhardy Arab grabbed at Jimbo and was slugged for his troubles. Another dived at Dead-eye and landed on his shoulders, but was spun off and crashed down onto a table under which some other Arabs were hiding. They all yelled and scattered around the falling man as he thudded into the ground.

As Dead-eye straightened up, having thrown off the Arab, he saw two others in suits standing near the dead man, spreading their legs to take aim with their pistols. Calling a warning to Jimbo as he prepared to shoot two-handed, Dead-eye fired at one of the two Arabs before either had managed a shot. His victim was jerking backwards, his pistol flying through the air, as Jimbo's Browning roared beside Dead-eye and the second Arab was also bowled over.

Still not recognized as British, they did not say a word, but turned away and ran as fast as they could along the narrow *souk*, following Terry. It was not a trading area, so they were relatively unhindered, and eventually, when they were sure that they were not being followed, they slowed down to a walk, gradually caught up with one another and walked together, like three Arab friends, to the car parked on the other side of Crater. Only when they were driving away did they let themselves relax, Terry and Jimbo whooping with pleasure while Dead-eye gazed out of the window, impassive and watchful.

'You should have seen the look on the face of that tourist,' Terry said, 'when I spoke to him in English. He couldn't believe it!'

'Must have nearly shit himself,' Jimbo laughed. 'I wish I'd seen his expression.'

'You're becoming too cocky for your own good,' Dead-eye said brusquely, 'and it's making you stupid. First you sit at a table where any Arab could have joined you; then you eat Arab food from a dirty portable stove; then, worst of all, you speak English in the vicinity of the Arabs. How fucking daft can you get? You forgot yourself, kid. Never do that again.'

Realizing that Dead-eye was right, Terry and Jimbo remained silent until the Q car was back in the safety of the military compound at Khormaksar. Terry spoke only when they had signed the car back in and were walking to the HQ tent to make their report.

'I'm sorry, Sarge,' he said to Dead-eye, looking suitably contrite. 'You were absolutely right.'

'No sweat, son,' Dead-eye said quietly.

Even before making their report to Lieutenant-Colonel Callaghan, Dead-eye and Jimbo were told by the RSM that they were being sent back to the squadron at Thumier for a major operation in the Radfan. Terry was going with them.

'Back where I belong,' Terry said. 'I'll be a good boy now.'

'I hope so,' Dead-eye said with the hint of a smile.

7

'Welcome back, gentlemen,' Callaghan said in his HQ tent in the base camp, shaking the three men's hands and indicating that they should take one of the hard wooden chairs facing his cluttered trestle table. 'I believe the Keeni-Meeni operation was a success.'

'Yes, boss,' Dead-eye said as he and Jimbo pulled up chairs and sat facing him. 'The two agents and a bodyguard were topped.'

'How was Trooper Malkin?'

'A bit on the cocky side, but he certainly knew what he was doing and did it precisely.'

Callaghan grinned at his squadron commander, Captain Ellsworth, sitting beside him. 'A bit full of himself, was he? Not grandstanding, I trust!'

'Not grandstanding, boss,' Dead-eye reassured him. 'Just thrilled to be showing two NCOs what to do. A little bit careless here and there from overconfidence, but he certainly proved that he'd learnt a lot during his couple of months with the Keeni-Meeni squads. He didn't let us down that way.'

'Maybe you should have left him in Aden,' Ellsworth said. 'Sounds like he belongs there.'

'It's too free and easy there, sir,' Jimbo explained. 'Terry works unsupervised. The work's dangerous, but being on his own – or with just a friend or two – makes it seem like a game. He's good, but he's still immature and needs to be brought back down to earth. So he's better off back here as part of the squadron. Besides, he's one hell of a signaller – practically psychic – so we wanted him back.'

Callaghan grinned again. 'Irish background, yes?'

'Right, boss. A bit of a Paddy. He doesn't like to be reminded of it, but that's what he is and the Paddy in him gives him great intuition when it comes to using the radio.'

'I don't believe what I'm hearing,' Captain Ellsworth said, shaking his head. 'You're saying that he has psychic abilities that help when it comes to communications?'

Jimbo was grinning now. 'I'm not saying it's

true, boss, but I *am* saying that a lot of the men believe that. They think Terry is an exceptional signaller because he's Irish and has psychic intuition. So they have confidence in him.'

Callaghan chuckled. 'Far be it from me to disillusion them. Fine. He's all yours.' He glanced up automatically when a great roaring passed overhead, indicating that a Wessex was coming in to land. He waited until the chopper had passed on and was descending on the nearby landing pad, then lowered his gaze again. 'So, gentlemen, let's get down to business. Now that those communist double agents have been removed, we can mount our operation in the Radfan without fearing that our every move is going to be telegraphed in advance to the enemy. In other words, you've just won yourselves some work.'

'Christ, boss, what's the second prize?' Jimbo said.

'It's mainly because of the machinations of those agents you terminated,' Callaghan continued in a serious vein, 'that our intelligence concerning the strength and whereabouts of the enemy in the Radfan is negligible. We don't know anything we need to know. We don't even know where there's water. We know precious little about the tribesmen. For this reason we want an improvised group to go back into the mountains and try to pick up as much information as it can, possibly even some prisoners. In fact, Captain Ellsworth has already done that once with a much smaller group.'

Both NCOs stared quizzically at the new, relatively inexperienced captain, who looked slightly embarrassed.

'It was in your absence,' Ellsworth said quietly. 'I took a small patrol up into the Radfan, set up a nocturnal ambush and opened fire on a camel train that refused to halt. A couple of Arabs were killed, but a third was taken prisoner. My initial anxiety was that I might have made a mistake – that the Arabs were legitimate traders. Luckily, when we brought our prisoners back down, a local military intelligence officer identified him as a known guerrilla leader.'

'Congratulations,' Dead-eye said.

'Well deserved, certainly,' Callaghan said. 'However, Captain Ellsworth's initial concern that he might have shot up a perfectly innocent camel train highlights one of the problems we have up there in the Radfan: it's swarming not only with the enemy, but with local traders going about their business – and if we shoot them by mistake it could lead to riots in Aden.'

'In other words,' Ellsworth said, 'we're going to have to be very careful before making any kind of move.'

'Dead right,' Jimbo said.

For a moment there was silence as Captain Ellsworth glanced thoughtfully at the map of the Radfan, spread out before him on the desk, and Callaghan gazed distractedly outside the tent, where the sun was sinking over the base camp, lengthening the shadows of the protective hedge-hogs and their armaments. The Wessex pilot had finally switched off his engines and the only sound now heard from the landing pad was the shouting of the ground crew and the lesser roar of a jeep starting up. The mountains of the Radfan, also visible through the opening in the tent, looked distant and mysterious in the dimming light.

'What kind of group are we taking up there?' Dead-eye asked.

'Two battalions of FRA infantry; 45 Royal Marine Commando with B Company; the Parachute Regiment; a troop of Royal Engineers; a battery of the Royal Horse Artillery armed with

105mm howitzers; and a Royal Tank Regiment equipped with Saladins.'

'That's not a small group,' Jimbo noted.

'No, Sergeant Ashman, it's not. But we don't know what we're up against, so we can't chance our arm.'

'What's the objective?' Dead-eye asked.

'Two hills, codenamed Rice Bowl and Cap Badge. Both are of vital importance because they dominate the camel routes from the Yemen and the only two fertile areas in the region. We intend to seize them from the rebels on 1 May.'

'Day or night?' Dead-eye asked tersely.

'To be caught in the valley in the daylight would be suicidal, so both of the assault forces will move out at night. The Royal Marines will march seven miles from the Dhala Road, in Thumier, into hostile territory, to climb and hold the most northerly objective – Rice Bowl. Simultaneously, the Para Company will be dropped by parachute near the foot of Cap Badge.'

Callaghan nodded at Ellsworth, who leant forward to say: 'This is where we come in. To land the Paras on an unmarked, undefended DZ would be just as suicidal as asking the Marines to march in broad daylight. Our task, then, is to establish, mark and protect a suitable DZ for the Paras.'

'What would they do without us?' Jimbo asked.

'How many men do we take, boss?' Dead-eye asked.

'Nine. You move out at dusk on 29 April, under the command of Captain Ellsworth and travelling in Saladins. You'll head due north along the Dhala Road, then leave the road at the Wadi Rabwa and climb up the sides of the wadi into the mountains. You'll have to cover approximately eight miles to reach your objective and you only have twenty-four hours to do so.'

'The opposition?' Jimbo asked.

'Intelligence reports suggest that it won't be serious if you move discreetly.'

'But, sir, you've just said,' Dead-eye reminded him, 'that intelligence about the Radfan is pretty thin – which means unreliable.'

The CO grinned and shrugged. 'What can I say, Dead-eye, other than what I've told you? Intelligence thinks you might get off lightly, but it could be the opposite.'

'Who dares wins,' Dead-eye said, staring out of the tent.

8

Late in the afternoon of the following day, the nine men selected for the patrol prepared to move out by camouflaging themselves and their weapons. Given the cramped size of the tents, most of them did this sitting outside in the mercifully falling temperature, with their weapons and kit spread around them. As usual, they first cleaned their weapons and checked the ammunition, which in this instance included four magazines for the SLRs, a total of eighty rounds, plus a bandolier of the same ammunition and 200 rounds of .303-inch bullets for the patrol's Bren gun. They were, in fact, more lightly armed than usual.

'Why?' Lance-Corporal Larry Johnson asked.

'Because Lieutenant-Colonel Callaghan prefers mobility to fire-power for this kind of operation,' Dead-eye informed him. 'That's why he also

136

stressed that our ammunition's to be conserved as much as possible, even during contact with the enemy. In other words, fire only when strictly necessary.'

'Like when I've got someone's bayonet up my arse?'

'That about sums it up,' Jimbo said.

When the weapons and ammunition checks had been made, they went off to collect their water ration: a one-gallon container and four water bottles per head. Now back doing what he was best at, Terry also collected his A41 tactical radio, which added another 44lb to his heavy load.

Finally, they darkened the exposed parts of the body – in particular the face, neck and hands – with stick camouflage. They also applied 'cam' to the shinier parts of the weapons to prevent them from reflecting the moonlight. Meanwhile the sun was setting beyond the mountains, and the hedgehogs around the perimeter of the camp, bristling with big weapons and howitzers, were receding into the gathering gloom.

'So what were you two doing when you were away?' Lance-Corporal Les Moody asked Deadeye and Jimbo.

'Not much,' Dead-eye replied.

'That isn't an answer, Sarge.'

'It was confidential,' Jimbo told him.

'But you were with little Terry here?' Les said, indicating the younger soldier with a nod of his head.

'That's right.'

'Which means you were in Aden.'

'You're so bright,' Jimbo said.

'I've heard that we have some special hit squads in Aden: blokes who dress up as Arabs and go into the *souks* for some close-action work with their 9-millis?'

'You've seen too many war films,' Jimbo said.

'I didn't pick it up there. That's the word going round.'

'Bloody rubbish,' Dead-eye told him.

'Is that right, Trooper?' Les asked Terry. 'Bloody rubbish?'

'You had it straight from the horse's mouth,' said Terry rather too curtly.

'Isn't it true that when you disappeared from the Sports and Social Club in Hereford it was to do a quick course in Arabic, then be flown to Aden for a couple of months with one of them Keeni-Meeni squads?'

'Keeni-Meeni?' Terry asked deadpan. 'What's that?'

'You don't know?'

Terry shook his head.

'That's bullshit, Terry. You know exactly what it means and it's what you were doing in Aden.'

'I was acting as a signaller in Aden and that's *all* I was doing. Isn't that right, Dead-eye?'

'That's right,' Dead-eye said.

'I can't get a straight answer to a simple question,' Les complained.

'Ask no questions and we'll tell you no lies,' replied Jimbo.

'My lips are sealed from this moment on,' Les said with a sigh.

They completed their preparations just as the sun was sinking. After heaving their bergens onto their backs, they strapped on their webbing and bandoliers of ammunition, then picked up their personal weapons and marched to the waiting Saladins. Apart from being equipped with 76mm QF guns and Browning .30-inch machine-guns, the armoured cars had been fitted in the manner of the World War Two LRDG Chevrolets, which were specifically equipped for the desert. Among the refinements were reinforced sand tyres, special filters, outsize fans and radiators, wireless sets, sun compasses, sextants, sand shovels, jerry cans, water condensers, woven sand mats and steel sand channels, the latter two to be used when the vehicle became trapped in sand or potholes. The sun had actually sunk when the armoured cars moved out of the camp one after the other.

As the convoy moved along the Dhala Road, into a deepening darkness relieved by moonlight and a sky perforated with stars, Terry glanced at the mountainous desert outside and thought how different it was from the terrain he had first fought in: the dense jungle and steaming swamps of Borneo. Though he had fought well there, earning his winged-dagger badge in no uncertain terms, he was still haunted by nightmares about how he and the rest of his squadron had waded through snake and insect-infested swamps, fighting Indonesian troops all the way.

While Terry's dreams were filled with vivid recollections of the snakes, bloodsucking leeches and countless insects of the stinking swamps, now they were even more frequently haunted by his vivid recollection of how he and a few of the others, including Dead-eye and Jimbo, had eventually been forced to cross an aerial walkway that swayed high above a roaring gorge and was being fired at by vengeful Indonesians. Even fully awake, Terry had only to close his eyes to see his friend, Trooper Pete Welsh, peppered by enemy bullets and pouring blood from his many wounds, slide off the bridge and fall screaming to the bottom of the gorge, where he splashed into the raging rapids, was smashed against the rocks and then swept away out of sight for ever. That sight, Terry was sure, would haunt him for the rest of his life.

The present terrain, though also mountainous, was very different from that of Borneo, being parched by the sun and filled with wide, open spaces instead of dense jungle. Yet it was just as dangerous, with its own brand of the unknown, and Terry was glad to be in the company of Dead-eye, who had successfully led him and the other survivors out of the swamps and mountains of Borneo.

Dead-eye was presently in one of the other Saladins, but Terry thought of him now because he was not feeling too good and thought he knew why. It was because, while in Aden with Dead-eye and Jimbo, he had being doing what both men detested: 'grandstanding'. This term, as

Terry knew only too well, was applied by the SAS to any soldier who forgot that he was part of a team and instead put on a show to earn credit or glory for himself.

Having been a newcomer in Borneo, constantly awed by the coolness and courage of the old hands, particularly Dead-eye, in Aden Terry had been unable to resist showing off to him and that other old-timer, Jimbo. He had sat at that café table in Crater and, even worse, eaten food from one of the notoriously unhygienic food stalls, purely as an act of bravado. It had also been an act of gross stupidity – for which he was now paying the price with an upset stomach.

Compounding his stupidity, he had not confessed before leaving the base camp that he had an upset stomach. Now that the convoy was in the middle of the desert, heading for Wadi Rabwa and the mountains beyond, Terry knew that he could not be taken back or casualty-evacuated. Unless he suffered in silence, he could become a serious burden to the whole patrol.

Unfortunately, his stomach, which at first had only been slightly upset with what seemed like mild indigestion, was now twitching constantly with sharp, darting pains and making him feel nauseous.

'How long's the drive?' Terry asked, glancing out of the Saladin at the vast flat plain running out to the distant mountains.

'We should be at Wadi Rabwa in less than an hour,' answered Jimbo. 'From there it's about eight miles to our objective, but we've got about twenty-four hours to get there. The wadi's pretty steep and the march will be rough. Why do you ask?'

Terry looked uneasy. 'My stomach's playing up,' he mumbled.

'What?'

'I feel queasy,' Terry confessed. 'But don't let on to anyone else. I don't want to be taken off the patrol.'

'How bad is it?'

'It hurts a bit and I feel sick.'

'You must have picked up a bug when you had that Arab food in Crater. That was daft, Trooper.'

'Yes, it was.'

'This is no time to be feeling sick.'

'I know. I'm really sorry, Sarge. I should have told you, but I thought it would go off soon.'

'But it hasn't?'

'No, Sarge.'

Jimbo sighed. 'You think you can stick with it throughout the hike?'

'I'll be OK. I promise.'

Jimbo shook his head in disbelief, then turned away. Squirming with guilt, Terry glanced at the other men in the armoured car – the recently badged troopers, Ben Riley and Taff Thomas – and was relieved that they appeared not to have heard the conversation.

'Are you two all right?' Jimbo asked them.

'Yes, Sarge,' Ben replied while Taff just nodded.

'You weren't the last time,' Jimbo reminded them.

'No, not the last time,' Ben replied in his cocky manner. 'We were only sick on the first trip, Sarge. That was in the middle of the day when the sun was as hot as hell. The last time, when we went out at night, like this, you had no problems with us.'

'I stand corrected,' Jimbo said, then yawned into his clenched fist.

Glancing at Ben and Taff, Terry remembered being told just how ill they had been shortly after arriving at Aden, on the drive from the RAF base in Khormaksar to the SAS camp in Thumier. Hearing about that journey had made Terry feel superior to the newcomers; and that sense of superiority, which he could now see as a weakness, is what had made him behave so badly in Crater, trying to impress his two more experienced sergeants. Now ill himself, he did not feel so superior to the two newcomers, and even felt ashamed.

Even more disconcerting was the knowledge that, while the journey so far had been along the Dhala Road, which was smooth enough, soon they would be leaving the road to ascend into, then climb out of, the steep rocky sides of Wadi Rabwa. After that, the going would be even rougher.

In fact, their descent into the eerily moonlit wadi began five minutes later when the Saladins turned off the road, bounced across very rough terrain, which jolted the vehicles relentlessly, then started inching down into the wadi with gears grinding and powerful engines screaming in protest.

At first the slope of the wadi could be seen in the moonlight, which streaked the loose grey gravel and parched, lunar rocks, but when they finally reached the dried-up watercourse, which ran for miles east and west, the moonlight was almost completely cut off by the opposite slopes and the column moved for a time through almost total darkness.

Time after time, the armoured cars ran into boulders too large to bounce over or became stuck in potholes too deep to traverse. When this happened, the men, guided by Jimbo, who had learned his desert skills with the LRDG in North Africa, had to climb out and either remove the boulders by hand or get the vehicle out of the large potholes with the aid of the woven sand mats or five-feet-long steel sand channels.

This latter operation involved pushing the sand mats or metal channels as far as possible under the wheels that had become stuck in the soft sand. The armoured car could then be either reversed or advanced slowly over them until it was free. A simpler variation on the original LRDG method of rescuing their Chevrolets from sand traps, it was effective but laborious and time-consuming.

Nevertheless, even in the pitch darkness, the men took the opportunity to check the tyres, usually letting some air out lest they burst on the sharper stones. They also checked that there was no sand in the carburettors. These tasks were managed by the light of hand-held torches.

This was a mistake. They realized so when, during an attempt to move another trapped vehicle, gunfire erupted from the hills beyond the wadi and a hail of bullets danced off the rocks nearby, causing pieces of stones to fly off in clouds of dust and showers of sparks.

'Shit!' Jimbo growled, dropping automatically to his knees and raising his SLR into the firing position. 'The bastards saw the torches.'

'Our own fault,' Dead-eye replied, dropping low beside him as the rest of the men scattered to take up firing positions from behind the armoured cars or higher rocks. He turned aside briefly to bawl at the men: 'Don't fire back! You'll be wasting your time. You'll only pinpoint our position. Just lie low and wait for further orders!' He was cut off when another burst of tracer made sand spit up in a jagged line that whipped and coiled nearby, causing more fragments of rock to fly up through clouds of dust and silver sparks that looked like fireflies.

Captain Ellsworth ran back from the first Saladin, crouched low, holding his SLR across his chest, as more green tracer from the enemy machine-guns looped languidly down from the distant hill, appeared to gain speed as it approached, then raced at him in a phosphorescent stream that made the soil explode in a jagged line behind him.

Falling to one knee beside Dead-eye, he stared at the lines of tracer and spitting sand. 'I thought the opposition wasn't going to be serious if we moved discreetly,' he said sarcastically.

'Shining torches at night isn't discreet,' Dead-eye replied.

'The enemy wasn't supposed to be here,' Jimbo reminded him. 'They're supposed to be in the Radfan.'

'That lot have come down from the Radfan,' Dead-eye said, 'and caught us all napping.'

'Caught us working our arses off,' Jimbo corrected him.

The combined firing of rifles and machine-guns on the distant hills was not all that loud from where they were, but once the bullets and tracers reached the area it became a clamorous combination of spitting, hissing, thudding and cracking, with the rocks making a sharp exploding sound when they were split by the bullets.

'I think we should keep moving,' Ellsworth said. 'It's pitch-dark in the bottom of this wadi and as long as we don't climb back up into the moonlight, they won't be able to see us.'

Given Ellsworth's relative inexperience, Dead-eye and Jimbo were both impressed and nodded in agreement. Then Dead-eye raised and lowered his right hand, indicating that the men should get back into their respective armoured cars. As they were hurrying to do so, a mortar shell exploded about

50 yards away, tearing the soil up in a mushroom of smoke and flying foliage, large stones, dust and loose gravel. The debris, when it rained back down, made an eerie hissing sound which grew louder as the roaring of the explosion faded away.

That first mortar explosion was followed by others as the last of the men were practically dragged into the Saladins and the column continued its tentative advance along the wadi without the benefit of lights. As the convoy left its original position, the enemy tracer and mortars spread out in a wider arc, moving away from the column in one direction, advancing towards it in another, indicating that the guerrillas were now firing blind, not knowing in which direction the column was moving and hoping to hit at least part of it by accident.

Luckily, the next time the lead vehicle, Ellsworth's, hit a larger boulder, the column was out of range of the enemy fire. But the tracer and mortar explosions continued to come nearer the column as the men in the captain's vehicle clambered out to roll the stone away. Even as he was directing two of his troopers in this difficult task, the darkness was brilliantly illuminated by the jagged flash of another exploding mortar, which showered the men in stones, gravel and swirling, choking sand.

Dead-eye materialized out of the settling cloud of sand, wiping some of it from his flat, grey eyes. He glanced back over his shoulder as more explosions erupted between the armoured cars and a hail of bullets ricocheted noisily off them. Turning back to Ellsworth, he said: 'I don't think we can make it any further in the Saladins. Those guerrillas will keep firing blindly down here until they hit one of us. When they do, the flames from the burning vehicle will light up the rest of us. I think we should make the rest of the journey by foot.'

'That's one hell of a hike, Sergeant.'

'Better than sitting here and being shot to pieces.'

More mortar shells exploded, one showering Ellsworth and Dead-eye with soil, sand and gravel. The captain glanced up at the dark hills, where he could see the minute flashes of the enemy rifles and machine-guns, then turned back to Dead-eye. 'I think you're right. We can move a boulder in the darkness, but we can't get an armoured car out of a pothole without using the torches, and that would be the end of us.' He nodded, covered his ears to shut out the roaring of another mortar explosion and clapped his hand over his face until the stinging, swirling sand and gravel had settled down, then said: 'Right. We'll hike out of here under covering fire from the Saladins' guns.'

While Ellsworth was telling the two troopers trying to move the boulder to forget it and get their weapons out of the armoured car, Dead-eye was making his way back down the line to tell the other men to do the same. Even before the first of them had climbed down, the 76mm QF guns and Browning .30-inch machine-guns of the armoured cars were roaring into life to rake the distant hills in the general direction of the flickering enemy guns.

Terry was one of the first out, jumping to the ground with his bergen on his back and his SLR in his right hand. Almost bowled over by the explosion from a mortar shell mere yards away, he staggered, steadied himself, ran through the hissing gravel and sand, then doubled up and vomited uncontrollably.

Gasping for breath, he glanced around to see if anyone had noticed. Relieved to see that the other men were too concerned with making their way between the explosions of the mortar shells and spitting lines of machine-gun fire, he knelt down, quickly wiped his boots clean with a paper hand-kerchief, then straightened up enough to run at the crouch towards the opposite side of the wadi.

Once there, Terry knelt beside Jimbo, Ben and Taff, all of whom were looking up to where the moon was lighting up parts of the steep, rocky slope. Feeling faint, but trying to hide it, he said: 'Well, are we going up or not?'

'Not much fucking choice,' Jimbo replied gruffly. 'Yes, Trooper, we're going up. Ready, lads?' They all nodded. 'Move out!'

With the Saladins' guns roaring in their ears, the men hurried up the lower slopes of the hill, soon leaving the explosions of the mortar shells and rebounding bullets behind them and melting into the moon-streaked darkness.

When the last of the men on foot had left the bed of the wadi, the Saladins turned around and went back the way they had come, keeping up a hail of fire in order to draw the attention of the guerrillas away from the troops scaling the rocky slopes. By the time the enemy guns had finally stopped firing – the guerrillas obviously convinced that they had forced a retreat – the SAS men had melted into the moonlit darkness above the wadi.

Silence enfolded them.

9

Halfway up the hill, the patrol turned east and headed away from where they had seen the guerrilla guns flickering. Adopting the diamond formation more suitable to open country, with Dead-eye out front on point and Jimbo acting as Tail-end Charlie, they marched through the moonlit darkness in silence. Even at night, the heat was stifling, making all of them sweat, but luckily this gave way to a comforting breeze as they climbed ever higher up out of the wadi.

It was not an easy march. Each man was still burdened down with his 60lb bergen, SLR and four magazines, plus a bandolier of the same ammunition and 200 rounds of .303-inch for the patrol's Bren gun, the latter weapon being carried between the even more heavily laden Ben and Taff. Each man also carried his full ration of water –

a one-gallon container and four water bottles per head. As for Terry, he was growing increasingly worried about having vomited, was not feeling any better for it, and soon began feeling exhausted from having to hump the additional weight of his A41 tactical radio.

By contrast, the other members of the patrol were in good spirits as they tramped between rocks and over the dunes of Wadi Rabwa. The higher they climbed, the more they were exposed to moonlight and the less dangerous the march became, given increased visibility. Nearing the top of the hill, they saw the mountains of the Radfan clearly, with the dark mass of the 3900-foot Jebel Ashqab soaring up to their right. Their objective lay on the other side.

The very thought of the climb was enough to fill Terry with fear. When he first saw the mountain, his stomach twitched involuntarily with nerves. This was followed by a spasm of darting pains that almost made him cry out, but he bit his lower lip and continued climbing in silence. His breathing was becoming more difficult and soon he was stopping frequently to fill his lungs.

By the time the patrol had climbed out of the wadi and was crossing open ground to the lower slopes of the Jebel Ashqab, Terry could hardly control the spasms in his guts and knew that he would have to throw up again. This he did after deliberately falling back to the rear of the column, forgetting that Jimbo was bringing up the rear a good distance behind the main formation. Terry was wiping his lips dry when Jimbo caught up with him.

'What are you doing here?' he asked, before seeing the mess around Terry's boots. 'Oh, Christ!' he said softly.

'Sorry, Sarge.'

'Too late for that, Trooper. You don't seem to be improving.'

'I'll probably be all right after this.'

'Let's hope so.' Still holding his SLR at the ready, Jimbo was glancing left, right and back over his shoulder as he talked, not forgetting the possible presence of the enemy and the constant need for alertness. 'All right,' he said, turning back to Terry, 'get back up there with the column. If you don't think you can cope, let me know. Meanwhile, I'll be watching you.'

'Yes, Sarge. Thanks.' Thoroughly ashamed of himself, Terry grabbed his SLR and hurried to catch up with the others and take his position at the rear of the diamond-shaped formation. He managed to keep up for another hour or so, but gradually fell behind again.

This time some of the other men saw him and automatically slowed down to let him catch up. At the head of the column, but well behind Dead-eye, who was still the scout, Captain Ellsworth saw something was happening and was about to make enquiries when Jimbo caught up with Terry and spoke quietly to him. Looking troubled even from where Ellsworth was standing, Terry wiped sweat from his face, adjusted the straps of his radio distractedly, then hurried to catch up with the rest of the men. When they saw him coming, they started off again and Ellsworth, deciding that, whatever was wrong, Jimbo must know what he was doing, marched on with them.

By now they were embarked on the even more arduous climb up the steep, rocky slopes of the mountain itself, where the loose gravel slid underfoot and patches of smooth lava gave way abruptly to sinking sand that could scarcely be seen in the darkness. More than one of the men tripped and fell, rolling downhill in a noisy tide of gravel until he was stopped by a boulder or the hand of a comrade. Others were visibly struggling for breath, owing to a combination of exertion and the night's stifling heat.

Given the problems faced by the healthier men, it came as no surprise to Jimbo when Terry vomited again, fell back again to catch his breath and caused the men nearest to him to stop and wait for him to catch up. This time, Jimbo called the patrol's medic, Lance-Corporal Larry Johnson, down the hill and told him to give the ailing trooper something for his stomach.

'What do you think caused it?' Larry asked, letting down from his shoulder his well-stocked medicine box.

'I don't know,' Terry said.

'Don't bullshit me, Trooper. I can't decide what to give you until I have a rough idea of what's wrong. Was it something you ate?'

'How would I know?' Terry responded, glancing anxiously at Jimbo.

The sergeant shook his head wearily. 'He had something from a food stall in Aden and I'm willing to lay odds that's what did it. Those carts aren't hygienic and he's not used to the food either. He's fucking well poisoned himself.'

Larry nodded. 'Bloody stupid thing to do,' he said, searching through the wooden box.

'I knew you'd say that,' Terry said.

'Not much else to say, is there, Trooper? Any stomach pains?'

'Yes.'

'Nausea?'

'Yes.'

'Fever?'

'I think so. We're all sweating so much climbing this mountain, I'm not sure.'

'Sweat's one thing; heat is another.' Larry placed his hand on Terry's forehead and cheeks. 'Fever. Diarrhoea or constipation?'

'I had pretty severe runs before leaving camp.' Larry glanced automatically at Jimbo. Terry, seeing the glance, hastened to explain: 'But it passed away the night before and I seemed to be all right the next day, which is why I didn't report it.'

'And now?'

'It seems to be constipation.'

'Which won't help your breathing.'

'I'm having trouble with that, too.'

Larry nodded. 'Food poisoning. I can't say how severe. I'll make you a little brew of tea, powdered charcoal and milk of magnesia.' Terry grimaced, but Larry, now grinning, continued: 'It tastes rotten, but it might absorb the poison in your stomach. I'll also give you some aspirin to bring down your fever. If neither remedy works, then the poisoning is severe and we've got problems.'

With the forward half of the patrol continuing to climb the mountain, unaware of what was happening behind them, the other troopers in the rear, not sure what to do, waited for Larry and Terry to finish what they were doing and catch up. Aware of this, Terry felt distinctly uncomfortable, but could only wait until Larry had mixed his potion in a metal cup and handed it to him. It tasted awful.

When Terry handed the cup back, Larry gave him two aspirins, poured some water into the same cup, handed it to him and told him to wash the tablets down. This was marginally easier than swallowing the first potion, but Terry literally took his medicine as punishment.

'If it gets worse, tell me,' said Larry, before packing his medicine box and hurrying back up the steep hill. Chastened, Terry glanced at Jimbo, who just nodded, grim-faced, indicating that he should follow Larry. When Terry had done so, the rest of the men began the climb again, now separated from the others by a large gap.

A cardinal mistake, Jimbo thought. *The guerrillas*

could use that gap to divide us and then we'd be finished. We can't continue like this.

Luckily, they were nearing the summit and the steep slope was gradually levelling out. Though it was still warm, a strong wind was blowing, moaning mournfully across the rolling hills and around the jagged peaks. Below, where the Wadi Rabwa cut through the flat desert, was almost total darkness, illuminated here and there by moonlight catching high rocks. It looked like a black sea of unknown depth.

Terry fell back again – and once more the men nearest to him waited for him to catch up while those in front kept marching, unaware that half of the column had stopped behind them. With another dangerous gap in the column having been created, Captain Ellsworth hurried back down the line to check what was happening.

'Trooper Malkin has an upset stomach,' Jimbo informed him, not mentioning the real reason. 'He must have picked up a bug and not known about it until we were well under way. He told me about it, boss, but by then it was too late to turn back the convoy. Lance-Corporal Johnson's already given him some medicine, but it doesn't appear to be working.'

Ellsworth studied the sweating, white-faced trooper. 'Is it bad?'

'Pretty bad, boss,' Terry readily confessed, grateful that Jimbo had saved his skin.

Ellsworth was about to say something else when Larry came back to join them.

'Still bad?' he asked, placing his hand on Terry's forehead to discover that it was still burning.

'Yes,' Terry said.

'Still feeling nauseous?'

'My stomach's settled down a bit, but I'm still having the pains.'

'Breathing problems?'

'Yes.'

Larry turned to the captain. 'He's suffering from food poisoning, boss. I was hoping it was mild, but I think we're out of luck. Not much I can do for him at the moment, except give him more of the same in the hope that it'll drain out some of the poison.'

'Assuming the second dose works,' Ellsworth asked, 'how long will it be before it takes effect?'

'A couple of hours.'

'So what do we do?' Ellsworth asked of Jimbo as Larry prepared another potion. 'We can't call in a CasEvac chopper and we can't leave him here.'

'Now that we're on the mountain and back in file formation, I suggest we put him in the middle of the file and redistribute the loads, with someone else carrying the radio. Lance-Corporal Moody's pretty good with it, so put him in charge of it.'

'Right, let's do that. Trooper, the radio.'

'But, boss . . .'

'Hand it over!'

Sighing deeply, Terry unstrapped the A41.

'I'll take that,' Ellsworth said. 'Signal when you're ready to move out. This delay has left a breach in the column and that could be dangerous.'

'Right, boss,' Jimbo said.

The captain marched back to the middle of the formation, as far as the gap, to give the radio to Les.

'Bloody typical!' Les complained quietly to his mate, Ken, when the captain had moved on to take up his position at the head of the second group. 'Malkin farts about in Aden, playing cowboys and Indians, then comes down with some bug that I'd bet he picked up from some filthy A-rab grub. They ought to RTU the little prick.'

'Difficult to RTU him from here,' Ken replied, grinning as Les strapped the radio onto his packed bergen. 'Anyway, that extra weight should do you good – keep the fat off you, mate.'

'Fuck you an' all, mate!'

When Larry had given Terry another dose of his potion, both men hiked back up to join the others. There, Terry was placed safely in the middle, so that he could be helped by the others should he falter. The patrol moved off again, the second half hurrying to catch up with the first.

Within half an hour it became clear that Terry was having even more difficulty breathing and was struggling even harder to keep up. At 0200 hours an exasperated Captain Ellsworth, increasingly worried about the gap being caused by Terry's erratic pace, called for a break and huddled down to confer with Dead-eye and Jimbo.

Though short of the precipice rising to the summit, they were now almost at the top of the highest ridge on Jebel Ashqab and, even better, sheltered from the wind by two ancient stone sangars that could only have been constructed as firing positions by local tribesmen.

'According to our original plan,' Ellsworth said, 'we were supposed to be in hiding on the objective before dawn, which is approximately 0530 hours. We'd then lie concealed until dusk, when we'd secure the DZ perimeter and identify it with torches and an Aldis lamp for the Paras' descent later that night. Unfortunately, Trooper Malkin's become a bit of a liability, dividing the patrol too often for my liking and also slowing us down considerably. At our present rate of progress, given the number of times we're having to stop, we won't reach the DZ on time. Any proposals, gentlemen?'

Dead-eye checked his logbook, then looked up again. 'According to my dead reckoning, we're still about three miles from the objective.'

'With this kind of climb, that's a long way. Now too long for us to get there by first light.'

'Right,' Jimbo said. 'And to be caught in the open after sunrise would make us soft targets for the guerrilla snipers hiding on the hilltops.'

'Which would compromise the entire operation,' Ellsworth said grimly.

They were silent for a moment. The captain stared moodily at the wall of the sangar, Jimbo peered over it at the hills silhouetted in the distance against the starry sky, and Dead-eye calmly studied his notes.

'It's not that bad,' he said eventually, raising his steady grey eyes to look directly at them. 'From here, it's all downhill to the DZ, which means we'll move quicker than we've been doing so far – even if we're held up again by Trooper Malkin. I estimate that we can cover the remaining ground at dusk tomorrow and still get to the DZ in time for the Paras' drop.'

Ellsworth nodded his agreement, then glanced around the sangar. 'Well,' he said, 'why not? If these sangars were built by tribesmen, the locals won't be suspicious if they see movement up here – they'll think we're Yemeni guerrillas. So, yes, Sergeant, let's basha down here until tomorrow night. That might also buy enough time for Trooper Malkin to recover.'

'This sangar's bigger than the other one,' Dead-eye observed, glancing over the wall at the sangar opposite, 'so we'll divide into two groups, one of four men, the other of five, and put the largest group in here.'

'That sounds sensible,' Ellsworth said. 'I'll stay here with the radio operator. You divide the rest up as you think best.'

'Corporal Brooke and Lance-Corporal Moody work well together, and since Moody's now got the radio, we'll put Brooke in here with you. As your second in command, I'll stay here as well. I don't think the smaller group should include someone as sick as Trooper Malkin, so we'll have him in here as our fifth man. Sergeant Ashman here . . .' – Dead-eye nodded at Jimbo – 'will be in charge of the other sangar, with Lance-Corporal Johnson and Troopers Riley and Thomas. The latter two will man the Bren gun.'

'Don't you think Johnson should be in with Trooper Malkin, to look after him?'

'No, boss. Johnson's already given Malkin his medicine and says it'll be a couple of hours before it takes effect – if it does. If it doesn't, on the other hand, the sangars are only a few feet apart, so we can get Johnson in here in seconds if the need arises. I think it's more important that the smaller group, being in charge of our sole machine-gun, is composed of healthy, alert men. So Malkin should stay here with us.'

'Fine,' Ellsworth said. 'Please attend to it, Sergeant.'

Dead-eye and Jimbo sorted the men into their two separate groups, each of which took over its own sangar: Captain Ellsworth, Dead-eye, Ken, Les and Terry in the larger one; Jimbo, Larry, Ben and Taff in the smaller.

'We always get the second-rate accommodation,' Ben groaned. 'That's 'cause we're the virgins.'

'They don't respect our finer qualities,' Taff agreed. 'They think we're second-class citizens.'

'You have a complaint, Troopers?' Jimbo asked, appearing out of nowhere and glaring at them.

'What's that, Sarge?' Ben asked, startled.

'Are you complaining about the sangar you've been placed in?'

'No, Sarge!'

'Absolutely not, Sarge!' Taff Thomas added.

'Good. I wouldn't like to think you were unhappy. I like to feel that my men are well pleased with the decisions I make. Otherwise, I'd be forced to put my boot halfway up your arseholes.'

'We're both fine,' Taff said quickly.

'Then get your lucky arseholes into that sangar and start setting things up.'

Once in their respective sangars, the men set them up like regular OPs, with rubber groundsheets rolled out for sleeping on, ponchos raised over the sangars and covered with loose gravel and vegetation, and a well for weapons dug out in the middle between the groundsheets. The men then tossed for who took the first watch and who the first nap. When this was decided, most of them settled in for the night, either sleeping or on sentry duty.

However, just before he lay down for his own three hours of sleep, Captain Ellsworth asked Les to contact Lieutenant-Colonel Callaghan in the Thumier HQ. When Les had done so, Ellsworth explained what had happened and what they planned to do. Callaghan, who had been in worse situations, swept Ellsworth's apologies aside and agreed that there was no alternative. He then told him to have a good sleep and wished him luck for the morrow.

The communication over, a more relaxed Captain Ellsworth sighed and settled down for the night. Though the air beneath the camouflaged ponchos was hot and stifling, he, like most of the men, slept well.

10

The sun rose at 0530 hours as an immense fiery
ball that poured what looked like lava along
the mountain peaks, increasing the temperature
and bringing with it the tormenting flies and
mosquitoes. In the morning's crimson-hued light,
the men awoke, yawned, rubbed their eyes and
joined the sentries at the wall, looking down the
hill to see an Arab hamlet a mere 1000 yards below
them. The hamlet was little more than a random
collection of mud-and-stone houses, with goats
tethered to posts, chickens cooped up in wire-mesh
cages, mangy, scavenging dogs, and Arab men and
women going about their morning chores.

'No guerrillas down there,' Captain Ellsworth
said.

'Yes, there are,' Dead-eye corrected him, pointing to the ridge directly above the hamlet, about

50 yards from the sangars, where armed men were tramping uphill to begin what would be a long day's watch.

'Damn!' Ellsworth whispered, as much embarrassed as surprised.

Annoyed to find that they were so close to a village held by the guerrillas, Dead-eye checked his map, then said: 'That must be Shi'b Taym.' Even as he looked up from the map, more guerrillas emerged from some of the primitive houses to eat breakfast around a communal table in the middle of the settlement, near what looked like a well. 'They're holding the village, all right.'

'Damn!' Ellsworth repeated, this time louder.

'Well,' Dead-eye said. 'Not much we can do except take notes, enjoy the scenery and wait for darkness to come. When it does, we can move out unseen.'

Ellsworth sighed. 'I suppose so.' Turning away from the wall to look at the other three men in the sangar, he saw that Terry still looked white and drawn. Ken and Les were making a brew-up with a hexamine stove and unwrapping their cold rations of dried biscuits and cheese. Terry was staring at the ground and licking his dry lips. 'How do you feel, Trooper?' Ellsworth asked.

'Not too good, boss.'

'Should we call Lance-Corporal Johnson over again?'

'I don't think he can do anything, boss. I haven't got diarrhoea and I'm not throwing up any more. It's these pains in my stomach, and I still feel pretty weak.'

Ellsworth glanced at the impassive Dead-eye, then turned back to Terry. 'Have you tried eating?'

The trooper nodded. 'I've tried, but I just can't stomach it. I'm all right until I think about food, then I feel nauseous.'

'He might be better off not eating,' Dead-eye said. 'Eating might start the runs or even make his pains worse. Whatever's wrong with him, no matter how bad it is, he'll just have to bear it until this is over and we're back at base camp. We can't call in a CasEvac.'

'No, I'm afraid not.' Ellsworth turned to Terry. 'But I think you should lie down, Trooper. Rest as much as possible.'

'Right, boss,' Terry replied, obviously relieved, before stretching out on the groundsheet in his shallow 'scrape' and rolling onto his side. He was still breathing harshly.

Turning away from Terry, Ellsworth and Dead-eye looked over the sangar wall. The guerrillas had taken up their lookout positions on the hills above the village and almost certainly could see the SAS men's sangars from where they were. Luckily, though, they were looking at their own rebel army's sangars and would not give them much thought so long as the SAS patrol stayed out of sight.

'Nice touch,' Ken said. 'We could stay here until the Millennium and they wouldn't know we were here. Perhaps we should pay them rent!'

The morning passed uneventfully. Down in the hamlet, the Arabs got on with their business, which consisted largely of feeding their goats and chickens, tending a small area of cultivated land, drawing water from the well and, judging from the smoke coming from various chimneys, lighting fires and cooking. Later some of the veiled women emerged to wash clothes in tubs placed in the middle of the village. The older men sat outside their houses, talking to each other, smoking from hookahs or surveying the empty desert and mountains.

'It's almost biblical,' Les said, taking a break from his radio to glance down over the wall.

'You'll see the parting of the waters any minute. Moses clutching the tablets.'

'I can't believe you've read the Bible,' Ken replied.

'I didn't,' Les replied. 'I saw the film. Cecil B. de Mille's *The Ten Commandments*. Fucking great, it was.'

'All that took place in Egypt,' Ken informed him. 'Not in this hell-hole.'

'Stick a pyramid down there and you'd swear it was Egypt,' Les said. 'Either that or a film set.'

'Get back to your radio,' Dead-eye barked, 'and stop distracting Corporal Brooke with your chit-chat. Corporal Brooke, you're supposed to be the sentry, so keep your eyes on that hamlet.'

'Yes, Sarge!'

'Daft fuckers,' Dead-eye muttered to himself.

In the early hours of the morning, the Arab children ran amok, playing in the dirt or chasing the dogs and goats; but later armed guerrillas emerged from one of the houses, organized them into a small group of three short lines, then marched them around the village clearing. Marching, the children chanted in unison: '*Allah yansir Nasir!*' ('God makes Nasser victorious!'), their voices shrill and pure, rising up clearly to the men hiding in the sangars. Dead-eye suddenly noticed that even the village elders had rifles beside them.

'That's a guerrilla village,' he said. 'They won't be on our side.'

'Let's remember that,' Ellsworth said.

Nevertheless, undetected as they were, they were able to relax, though Les explored the frequencies on his radio, trying to pick up enemy communications, Ken kept his eyes on the guerrillas on the hill opposite, and Dead-eye carefully entered in his logbook everything that was taking place down in the village. He even noted the exact time when the marching, chanting children were disbanded by their guerrilla trainers and allowed to return to their playing. When they did so, the silence returned, broken only by the odd shout of a guerrilla, a burst of laughter from one of the women around the wash tubs, or the barking of the dogs.

The morning passed slowly. By 1100 hours the sun was high in the sky, making the air beneath the camouflaged ponchos hot and stifling. Sweating profusely, the men were attacked by increasing numbers of buzzing, blue-bodied flies and whining mosquitoes. Drifting in and out of sleep, Terry dripped sweat and often groaned and slapped weakly at the insects. The other men cursed and swatted repeatedly at the same, though this merely agitated the insects and made them attack all the more frantically.

By noon the men could smell themselves and the air was even hotter and claustrophobic. Half an hour later the silence below the sangar was broken by the tinkling of small bells. Glancing down, Captain Ellsworth, Dead-eye and Ken, who were peering through the space between the ponchos and the top of the sangar wall, saw a herd of goats approaching along a small wadi only a few feet from the two sangars. The animals were being guided by a herdsman who shouted to a woman coming up the hill, telling her to watch out for the strays. The herdsman, however, apart from his walking stick, also had a .303 Lee-Enfield bolt-action sniper rifle slung over his shoulder.

'Not just your average villager,' Ken whispered as he studied the herdsman. 'That bastard's a Yemeni guerrilla.'

'Correct,' Dead-eye said.

They were joined at the wall by Les. As if communicating telepathically, the four of them cocked and raised their SLRs at the same time, covering the herdsman as he continued advancing up the hill. Thankfully, the woman to whom he was calling out was a good distance behind him, still practically at the bottom of the hill, at the hamlet's unfenced edge.

'He's getting close,' Ellsworth whispered to Dead-eye.

'Yes, boss.'

'We could do with a prisoner for interrogation. Could we grab him without causing a fuss?'

'Hardly, boss. His girlfriend down below would see everything.'

Ellsworth sighed. He then signalled by hand for the others to be silent, as the herdsman was now very close to the other sangar. Though he saw no movement from there, he knew that Jimbo would be on the alert and that Ben and Taff were probably already keeping the man covered with the Bren gun.

There was nothing for it but to wait and pray that the herdsman would not come close enough to spot them.

'If that bastard . . .' Ken was saying when suddenly the herdsman stopped, studied the two sangars, then bawled a warning to the woman below. Even as he turned to run back down the hill, unslinging his Lee Enfield on the move, the woman let out a demented falsetto wail that cut the silence like a knife and was clearly a warning to the guerrillas down in the village.

'Fuck!' Dead-eye whispered. 'The game's up.'

Foolishly, the running herdsman stopped briefly to turn back and take aim with his rifle. A single, high-velocity shot exploded in Ellsworth's right ear. Startled, he glanced sideways and saw Dead-eye squinting along the sight of his SLR, which now had smoke drifting out of its barrel. Ellsworth glanced down again as the herdsman, slammed backwards by Dead-eye's bullet, dropped his rifle and then fell and rolled further down the hill in a shower of gravel and sand.

As the woman continued her eerie, high-pitched wailing, meanwhile running back towards the hamlet, armed guerrillas burst from some of the hovels, fanning out as they ran, and started up the lower slopes, firing their rifles as they advanced. The woman threw herself to the ground as her comrades' bullets whistled over her head and bounced off the two sangars.

The Bren gun in the smaller sangar roared into action, tearing up sand and soil in a jagged, dancing line that first cut across, then through, the ranks of advancing guerrillas, making some of them shudder violently and fall over. The roar of the combined fire of the SAS small arms was added to that of the light machine-gun, creating even more havoc among the advancing guerrillas. More died, and others were wounded. The screams of the latter cut through the gunfire. The other guerrillas spread out over a wider arc and advanced uphill by darting from one rock to another under the covering fire of their comrades. Eventually, however, pinned down by the fusillade from the SAS guns, they had to content themselves with taking pot-shots from behind the boulders. Though they did not hit any of the patrol, they came close many times.

'We can keep them pinned down from here,' Ken said. 'No problem at all. The minute they stick their turbaned heads up, we can take their heads off, turbans and all. They can't do too much down there.'

At that moment, however, the guerrillas watching from the opposite ridge also opened fire with their rifles. Given that the ridge was only 50 yards away from the sangars and 20 feet higher, they could survey the whole sweep of the ground and aim with great accuracy. Their bullets ricocheted off the walls of both sangars, fragmenting the rocks and filling the space inside with boiling dust and flying pieces of sharp stone that cut like razors.

'Damn!' Ellsworth exploded, twisting away from the wall and covering his face with his hands until the first burst of enemy gunfire had subsided. Removing his hands and wiping dust from around his eyes, he said to Les: 'Get in touch with Thumier and arrange for some air support to deal with that ridge. Once that's done, we can tackle the men below.'

'Right, boss.'

'Jimbo!' Dead-eye bawled at the second sangar during a brief lull in the firing.

'Yes, Dead-eye!' the cry came back.

'You all right over there?'

'No problem. We're all hale and hearty. Ready, willing and able.'

'Good. We're calling up air support.'

'Bloody right!' Jimbo shouted. 'That fucking ridge is going to do us all in.'

'In the meantime, I want you to keep that ridge covered with the Bren and everything else you've got. We'll concentrate on the ones below.'

'Hear you loud and clear, Dead-eye. Over and out!'

No sooner had Jimbo gone silent than the Bren

gun, manned by Ben and Taff, roared into life again, turning the higher slope of the opposite ridge into a convulsion of spitting soil and spiralling dust that obscured the enemy and temporarily made them keep their heads down. While the two troopers kept up a constant fusillade, Jimbo and Larry gave them support with their SLRs, adding to the hellish destruction on the ridge facing them.

'Here they come!' Dead-eye bawled, lowering the barrel of his SLR and squinting down the Trilux sight and foresight at the Arabs below him. With the Bren gun now concentrating on the ridge, the guerrillas on the slopes below had decided to tackle the hill again and were advancing, as before, by flitting expertly from one rock to another, firing only when safely shielded.

'Conserve your ammo,' Dead-eye reminded the others. 'Fire only when you've got a specific target. We don't know how long we're going to be trapped here, so every bullet counts.'

A fluttering *shemagh* was just about all Dead-eye saw of an Arab who suddenly jumped up from behind a rock and dashed in a cloud of dust towards another. But that was enough. With the speed and accuracy he had perfected in South-east Asia, Dead-eye switched to single shot, squeezed the trigger once, and put a bullet into his target's head. The guerrilla spun away from him, his head jerking violently sideways, his rifle spinning to the ground as his hands clawed at the air, trying desperately to grasp something as the real world dissolved. He fell twisting like a corkscrew, already dead meat and bone, and had barely thudded into the ground when another Arab jumped up and ran.

Dead-eye and Ken fired at the same time, both on single shot. The guerrilla's head jerked to the left, his body twisted to the right, and he dropped his rifle to claw frantically, disbelievingly at his wounds – one hand on his bloody chest, the other covering his shattered head – and then went into a St Vitus's dance and fell face first in the dust.

Some of the Arabs behind the rocks, incensed by the deaths of their comrades, leant out recklessly and fired a few shots. The bullets zipped off the sangar walls, splitting chips off the stones and filling the air with choking dust; but even before the dust cleared Dead-eye and Ken were firing again, keeping the Arabs pinned down. While the two were thus engaged, Captain Ellsworth was kneeling on the ground beside Les, who, having made radio contact with Thumier, was looking enquiringly at his CO.

'You have a link-up?' Ellsworth asked, shouting above the roaring of the guns from both sangars.

'Yes, boss. I've got Major Williamson on the line.'

Relieved, Ellsworth relayed his request for air support to the SAS second in command at HQ. He then turned back to look over the sangar wall at the lower slopes of the hill, where bullets from the SLRs of Dead-eye and Ken were making soil and sand spit heavenwards between the rocks shielding the guerrillas.

'You got through?' Dead-eye asked.

'Yes.'

'How long will they take to get here?'

'Half an hour, I should think,' Ellsworth replied sardonically. 'Apart from the time required for the flight, communication won't be that immediate. First, my message to the SIC at Thumier will have to be amplified by a civilian radio transmitter. It'll then be relayed by field telephone to the RAF Brigade Air Support Officer in another tent. With a telephone in one hand and a microphone in the other, the Air Support Officer will then repeat my request, with specific fire orders, to the Hawker

Hunters at RAF Khormaksar. Add fifteen minutes for take-off and the flight and you have a fair estimate.'

'I'm encouraged,' Dead-eye said.

Ellsworth's estimate was fairly accurate. The first pair of RAF Hawker Hunter F Mark 6 single-seat fighters appeared over the southern horizon about thirty minutes after contact had been made. As more enemy rifle fire struck the sangars from the top of the ridge and the lower slopes below them, the Hunters roared down with guns chattering savagely, wreaking devastation on their positions on the opposite ridge.

The ridge exploded in geysering soil and boiling dust, with foliage, gravel and splintered stones hailing all around the men trying desperately to make their escape. The ground erupted between them, one explosion following another, and soon the summit of the ridge was obscured completely in a dark pall of smoke, falling debris and drifting dust.

The screaming of the wounded reverberated around the hills. Arab voices were shouting frantically, calling to one another to verify who was still alive, who was wounded and how many were dead. When the dust settled down, the surviving guerrillas had fled back down the hill to the comparative safety of the rocks on the lower slopes surrounding the hamlet.

Unable to attack the other guerrillas on the slope directly below Ellsworth's position, the Hunters flew in low over the sangars, saluting the SAS, then turned back and headed for home.

'Jesus!' Ken whispered, taken aback by what he had just seen. Returned to consciousness by the noise, Terry merely looked around him, bewildered, then groaned and closed his eyes again. Ellsworth and Dead-eye, elbow to elbow, stared down the hill.

So violent had been the attack that the dust and smoke over the ridge began drifting down over the hamlet, where the women and children were emerging from their huts to gaze up in fear and awe. At the bottom of the slope, where the other guerrillas were still in hiding, one of them, enraged by the fighter attack, stood up in full view, roared a stream of abuse in Arabic, then raised his rifle to fire.

Dead-eye's SLR spoke first. The guerrilla was thrown back into the dirt as if floored by an invisible fist. Within seconds a fusillade of rifle fire aimed at the sangars tore the silence apart.

Ellsworth and Dead-eye lowered themselves behind the wall as bullets whistled over their heads and ricocheted off the rocks of the sangar wall, filling the stifling space with flying fragments of rock and choking dust.

'At least they'll stay off that ridge,' Ellsworth said, wiping dust from his eyes and lips, 'which means they won't be overlooking us. If they want us, they'll have to come up the hill, and that won't be that easy.'

'It won't be that hard, either,' Dead-eye said in his icily realistic way. 'The survivors from the ridge are joining the others at the bottom of the hill. I think we're in for a tough fight.'

When a low, choked, moaning sound filled the gloom of the sangar, they all looked down at the single shallow scrape near their feet. Terry was tossing and turning on his groundsheet, deathly white, pouring sweat.

'This is bad,' Ken whispered.

11

As the guerrillas flushed out from the devastated ridge moved east to join those hiding on the slopes of the southern hill, it became obvious to Ellsworth and Dead-eye that this conflict was not over by a long shot. In fact, as the first two Hunters disappeared over the horizon, heading back to Khormaksar, the growing numbers of guerrillas behind the rocks below began to spring up and fire rapid single shots, targeting anything they could see moving between the camouflaged poncho sheets and the top of the sangar walls.

The Arabs were good, and though they scored no direct hits, they repeatedly sent fragments of shattered stone into the faces of the SAS men whenever one of them attempted to peer over the sangar wall. After half an hour, both sangars were filled with choking dust and no man had escaped being bruised or cut. Their situation was made all the worse by the growing heat and the buzzing, whining insects, oblivious to the exploding rocks and thickening dust.

Each time a fresh round hit their position, the men in the two sangars would call out to one another, checking that everyone was all right. They also joked to keep up their sinking spirits. But, try as they might, they found it hard to see just where the shots were coming from, as by now the Arabs, more numerous every minute, were running to and fro, changing positions, and only popping up long enough to get off another round. The SAS men were encouraged when a second pair of Hunters appeared overhead. Guided down by the identification panels originally intended for the DZ and now spread out on the ground between the sangars, they wheeled and dived repeatedly on strafing runs that raised a maelstrom of dust, sand and debris around the Arabs, yet, amazingly, failed to dislodge them from their hiding places, from where they continued to fire single shots up the hill.

'Tenacious bastards,' Ken murmured, then raised himself slightly, squinted down through his Trilux sight, and fired off a couple of bursts of his SLR. He had the satisfaction of seeing an Arab throw up his arms in a convulsion of dust raised by the bullets, then drop his rifle and fall back behind the rock.

While the sniping match continued, with Dead-eye and Ken doing the shooting from the larger sangar, Terry continued to writhe in fever, unconscious but groaning. Captain Ellsworth, through Les, concentrated on getting messages to the Hunters, correcting their course during the run-ins to strafe the guerrillas.

'You're doing a good job there, boss,' Ken said.

The captain nodded his gratitude as he squinted intently at the strip of silvery-blue sky visible through the gap between the poncho and the top of the wall. Yet even as the RAF fighters were pounding the guerrillas below, Dead-eye saw more of the enemy coming over the ridge and making their way down through the smoke-filled hamlet, where the women and children were still outdoors, watching the fight as if at a fair. Once through the hamlet, the guerrillas made their way up the southern slope to join the others behind the rocks.

The rifle fire from below was becoming more intense, though Ben and Taff, in the smaller sangar, were keeping most of the Arabs pinned down with a ceaseless fusillade from the Bren gun, supported by Jimbo and Larry's SLRs.

'It's not enough,' Dead-eye observed. 'Those Arabs below are too close to us to be bombed, but we must stop any more guerrillas coming over that ridge. There must be a camp on the other side.'

'Artillery support?' Ellsworth asked.

'I think so,' Dead-eye said. 'I'd also ask for some more Hunters to locate the enemy camp on the other side of that ridge and give it a pounding.'

'Will do,' Ellsworth said.

The artillery strike was called up in the early afternoon and the explosions soon turned the sunlit ridge and the area beyond it into a hell of boiling smoke streaked with crimson and yellow flames. Even as a great mushroom of smoke was forming over the ridge, another couple of Hunters were flying above it to wheel and dive repeatedly on the camp they had obviously found at the other side. The noise of the explosions, combined with the savage chatter of the guns of the fighters, was deafening and nerve-racking, making the guerrillas further down the slope stop firing to look up in fearful awe at the ridge.

The SAS men cheered. Enraged by this, the

SOLDIER J: SAS

guerrillas behind the rocks opened fire once more
with their rifles, now determined more than ever
to get the accursed Englishmen off the hill. But
though the Hunters continued to fly in on strafing
runs against the snipers, they were becoming less
effective as the sun set and the guerrillas were
gradually coming closer, making their way, rock
by rock, up the hill. As the sun sank low in the sky,
the shadow of the east side of Jebel Ashqab crept
over the sangars, then over the boulders below,
where the guerrillas were sheltering. It would soon
be dark.

'We'll lose our air support completely at last
light,' Dead-eye reminded Captain Ellsworth. 'Those
guerrillas haven't given up on us; they're just biding
their time. Given the bashing they've taken and the
destruction of their camp, they'll have a few debts
to collect. They don't intend letting us escape.
They're just waiting for darkness.'

But they did not wait. About half an hour later,
clearly still angry at the bombing and frustrated
that they could not dislodge the English soldiers,
a group of guerrillas sprang out from behind their
shelters and began a serious attempt to climb the
hill, sprinting from one rock to the other, firing
on the move, and covered by a murderous hail

of fire from those still in hiding. So intense was the covering fusillade that both sangars became alive with exploding pieces of rock and dust, the men inside scarcely able to pop up long enough to return a single shot. All of them, including the delirious Terry, were cut by pieces of stone and choked by the dust. But Ken was the first to be actually wounded by a bullet, instinctively letting loose a cry of pain and clutching at his left leg.

'Shit!' he muttered, swiftly regaining control of himself and gritting his teeth. He examined his leg, saw his trouser leg soaked in blood, explored tentatively with his fingers, winced twice, then said: 'Fuck it. I've got two bullets in my left thigh. What a bloody mess!'

The Bren gun roared from the smaller sangar, cutting a swath through the advancing guerrillas, bowling quite a few over, and eventually forced the others to go to ground once more. Just as it stopped roaring, however, to enable Taff to put in another belt, Ben called out to Captain Ellsworth: 'I've been hit, boss!'

'Ben's been hit as well!' Ken echoed mockingly, despite his own pain.

'Shit!' Ben cried out in fear and shock through a

lull in the firing, ignoring Ken's remark. 'My back stings like hell!'

'The round crossed his back,' Larry explained encouragingly to Captain Ellsworth, also shouting between the two sangars, 'leaving a wound like a whiplash. It'll hurt, but he's OK. What about you, Corp'?'

'Two bullets in the fleshy part of the left thigh,' Ken bellowed above the renewed noise. 'It's bleeding a lot.'

It was also hurting badly, but he did not mention that fact. He examined the wounds carefully, his fingers soaked in blood and torn pieces of flesh, pressing here, pinching there, grimacing with pain, but still trying to discover just how bad the wound was.

'I think I've been lucky,' he said to the concerned Captain Ellsworth while Dead-eye jumped up to fire at a running Arab. 'The bullets are .303-inchers, but they're actually refills.'

'Pardon?' Ellsworth asked as Dead-eye's single shot made the running Arab stop, jerk upright, drop his weapon and fall back heavily into the dust.

'Refills,' Ken repeated, removing his dripping fingers from the sticky mess visible through his torn OGs. 'Old shell cases filled with a home-made charge. The velocity isn't great enough to penetrate bone. These wounds are pretty bad, but at least they're only flesh wounds. I'm not finished yet, boss.'

'Good man.' Ellsworth patted Ken on the shoulder, then glanced down the hill where another Arab was at that moment jerked off his feet by another single shot from Dead-eye's SLR. The guerrillas had settled down again and their covering fire had tapered off temporarily.

'Corporal Brooke!' Larry called out from the smaller sangar.

'Yes?'

'I'm going to throw over some extra field dressing weighted with a stone. Make sure someone catches it. Can you bandage yourself?'

'Yes.'

'Here it comes.'

As the extra dressing sailed through the air, from one sangar to the other, Les jumped up and grabbed it, and dropped down again beside Ken.

'Nice catch,' Ken said. He took the bandage from Les, examined it, then shouted over the sangar wall: 'Is this the best you can do after that expensive stint at the US Army Training School in Houston?'

'Any more remarks like that and I'll come over there and cut off that leg.'

'Sincere apologies, Lance-Corporal.' Tearing away the blood-soaked, torn cloth from the two bullet wounds, Ken studied the blood-filled holes with a cool eye. 'Not nice,' he murmured.

Sliding down beside him to examine the wound, Dead-eye said: 'You'll need a tourniquet as well as a bandage. Those wounds are bleeding too much.'

'I reckoned that,' Ken replied.

Dead-eye offered a rare, fleeting grin. 'Can you do it yourself?'

'Yes, Sarge. No sweat.'

'They're coming up the hill again!' Jimbo bawled from the other sangar.

The Bren gun roared into life again as Captain Ellsworth and Dead-eye glanced down through the slit between the poncho above them and the top of the wall. Again, the guerrillas at the front – at least a dozen of them – were making their way up the hill by darting from rock to rock under the covering fire of their comrades lower down, now lost in the gathering dusk. As Ellsworth glanced automatically at Les's radio, instinctively thinking of air support, Dead-eye poked the barrel of his SLR through the slit and began picking the guerrillas off one by one.

'Damn!' Ellsworth said, glancing back down the slope to confirm that darkness was falling rapidly. 'It's too late for air support.'

'Correct,' Dead-eye replied, still squinting through the sight of his SLR and felling the running guerrillas with unerring accuracy.

With no immediate need for the radio, Les picked up his SLR and started rising to his knees to join Ellsworth and Dead-eye at the firing slit. At that moment, the rifles giving covering fire to the guerrillas roared in a sustained burst. A couple of bullets penetrated the sangar and ricocheted from one side of it to another. Les yelped and collapsed, clutching at his right leg. Twisting around, he saw that he had been hit in the thigh, like Ken, but with only one bullet. Although the pain gave way to numbness almost immediately, blood spurted from the wound with the force of water from a burst pipe. Les quickly covered it with his hand, while reaching into the survival belt with the other for a bandage.

'Bloody 'ell!' he exclaimed softly, tentatively

touching the red-fringed hole with his fingers and feeling nothing at all. 'Welcome to the club.' Ken, propped up against the sangar wall beside Ellsworth and Dead-eye, covered in dust and pieces of gravel and stone, with his wounded leg stretched out in front of him, grinned at the remark. Grinning back, trying to make light of their common situation, Les expertly bandaged his own wound, then tried moving his leg. 'Can't feel it, can't move it,' he said. 'No use at all.'

Dead-eye stopped firing at the guerrillas long enough to glance back over his shoulder at Les, who was tentatively pressing the foot of his wounded leg against the wall.

'I can't support myself on this,' Les said.

'That could be fatal,' Dead-eye replied in his pragmatic way. 'If you can't make that leg function by dusk, you'll stay here as dead meat.'

'Thanks a lot, Sarge!'

'Get it working, Lance-Corporal. Keep exercising it. Don't stop until you get feeling and strength back into it. If feeling comes back into it, it'll hurt, but you'll just have to ignore that. Either you march out of here or you stay here and die. So get exercising.

Desperate to have the leg working before the

patrol moved on, Les lay there and started pressing his foot against the wall, over and over, while bullets flew off the sangar wall and filled the air inside with a fog of dust.

Within minutes another bullet whizzed from one side of the sangar interior to the other and grazed the inside of Les's good leg, making him yelp with pain again.

'Christ!' he burst out, examining the slight graze. 'Nearly lost my balls that time!'

Ken chuckled as he sat upright against the wall, testing his own wounded leg and becoming confident that he could walk on it, no matter how painful.

'Your voice went up a few octaves there,' he said. I thought you *had* lost your balls.'

'That's just jealousy and wishful thinking, mate. It's just a graze. I'm all right. At least *this* leg is. It's the right one that bothers me.'

As the battle raged, Les kept testing his leg against the sangar wall. Gradually, feeling returned, bringing excruciating pain with it.

'Christ, it hurts!' he muttered.

'At least now you know you've got it,' Ken replied. 'Thank the Lord for small mercies.'

Wincing with pain, Les picked up his SLR and

turned to the front. At that moment the guerrillas attempted to rush the sangar. In the half light of dusk, partially obscured by the dust kicked up by their running feet, and with their *futahs* and *shemaghs* flapping, they looked like ghosts. They were real enough, though, as was proven when they screamed, quivered and fell, cut down by the Bren gun and sustained small-arms fire of the SAS.

The enemy were now very close and two of them had actually reached the wall of the larger sangar and attempted valiantly to push it over. This was brave, but unwise. Dead-eye and Les stood up simultaneously, the latter ignoring the pain in his wounded leg, and fired short, lethal bursts into the guerrillas, who quivered epileptically, their robes torn to shreds and soaked with blood, then fell back into the billowing dust.

Two more short bursts tore through the other guerrillas, killing some, wounding others, and the remainder fled back down the hill, leaving their dead, but dragging the screaming wounded with them. Before they could be shot at, Dead-eye and Les dropped back into the sangar, leaning against the wall and squinting through the deepening, dust-filled darkness at their ghost-like comrades.

Captain Ellsworth was squatting beside the groaning, restless Terry while Ken, his eyes gleaming sardonically out of circles of dust, methodically exercised his wounded leg.

Sighing, Ellsworth left Terry and returned to the firing slit of the sangar to look down over the wall. The guerrillas had fled back down the hill and could not be seen in the darkness. They had dragged away their wounded, but the dead still littered the moonlit slopes, some so dusty that they resembled the rocks about them. The dust, which was still blowing over them, took the shape of spectral figures and moaned softly, eerily. There was no other sound.

'It's time to leave,' Dead-eye said, brutally breaking the silence.

12

'That was Lieutenant-Colonel Callaghan,' Captain Ellsworth said, handing the microphone of the A41 back to the wounded Les Moody. 'He's just confirmed what we already knew: air cover has been called off for the night. We're all on our own now.'

He glanced down over the wall of the sangar, but saw only moonlight gleaming on the smooth volcanic rock between patches of sand on the slope that ran down to the hamlet. Though seeing nothing else, he knew, as did the others, that the guerrillas were still down there, preparing to move against the sangars. Indeed, they were probably advancing right now by moving stealthily from rock to rock under cover of darkness.

Turning back to his men, he said: 'Might as well admit it. Our original plan to mark the Paras' DZ has gone for a burton. All we can do now is attempt to break out and make our way back to Thumier. There's not going to be a rendezvous, so we might as well get on with it.' Then, as if unable to hold in his frustration, he added explosively: 'What a bloody disaster!'

'Like this whole bloody war,' Ken said, forlornly studying his wounded leg. 'A complete waste of time from start to finish. Lost before it began. Bloody politicians!'

No one said anything, but they all agreed with him. This was one of the few engagements they had been in that had given them no sense of pride or achievement. As their squadron commander had told them, this war was a lost cause created by politicians intent on getting Britain out of the colony while leaving a British presence there at the same time. That remaining presence, of which the SAS was a small part, had the least enviable job of all: defending a people who did not want to be defended and increasingly supported the so-called enemy. Most of the men felt bitter about this and, rather than taking pride in what they were doing, just wanted to do their best while stuck there and get the hell back home as soon as possible. It was not a good way to fight.

'Anyway, Callaghan agrees that we should try to break out and he's arranged to send in another troop by helicopter, to lend us support. That chopper is already on its way and should be here soon. Meanwhile, we wait. Sergeant Parker?'

'Yes, boss,' Dead-eye said from his position at the sangar wall, where he was keeping his eye on the moonlit slope with the aid of his night-vision goggles.

'Any sign of movement down there?'

'Not yet – though I suspect they're on the move. That chopper had better come soon.'

'Indeed it had, Sergeant. Keep your eyes peeled. What about you men? Are you all right?'

'Absolutely fine, boss,' Ken replied laconically, looking down at his bandaged, bloody leg, then glancing across at his similarly wounded friend. 'I've done my left leg, Lance-Corporal Moody's done his right, and Trooper Malkin's practically delirious with an upset stomach and a raging fever. Apart from that, we're fine, boss.'

'Do you think you can make it out of here?'

'Yes, boss. Both of us can just about walk and we'll do anything – and I mean *anything* – to get the hell out of here. As for Trooper Malkin, though, I've got my doubts ...' He glanced sideways to where Terry was stretched out in his shallow scrape, no longer tossing and turning on his rubber groundsheet because he was now too weak for even that. 'What the hell do we do? The kid's out like a light. Les and I can just about walk – we can't carry Terry. That leaves you and Dead-eye. But if you carry him, boss, you can't use your weapons.'

'We'll carry him if it kills us,' Dead-eye said.

'It just might,' Ken replied. While they waited for the chopper to arrive with the support team, he checked his wounded leg again, tested it against the wall of the sangar, and thought about how nice it would be to be back in Blighty with the Beatles and the Rolling Stones on the radio and all the girls in their miniskirts. It was a good time to be in England, Ken reckoned. He wanted to sit in front of the television, watching the amazing Cassius Clay bring down the lumbering Sonny Liston or, even better, the sexy Christine Keeler and Mandy Rice-Davis bring down a government or, almost as good, the unfolding tale of the Great Train Robbers, who were fast becoming heroes to the British public. He wanted desperately to visit his local and have a pint of decent bitter, read about the antics of Peter Sellers and Britt Ekland in the

Sunday papers, or the fights between Mods and Rockers. Or simply listen to Radio Caroline.

What he did not want to listen to was a lot of stuck-up, self-serving politicians spouting about Aden, Cyprus, Israel, Rhodesia, South Africa or Uganda; or about the fact that they were planning to waste £160 million of taxpayers' money on building a totally unnecessary Channel Tunnel. Who wanted the Frogs on their doorstep?

Ken glanced at Terry, saw that he was still ivory-white, sweaty and unconscious, though mumbling constantly to himself in his delirium, and wondered how the hell they could get him out. Bad enough that he and Les had leg wounds; Terry just made it worse.

He was distracted by the sound of an approaching helicopter. Glancing up, he saw a Wessex S-58 Mark 1 emerge from the southern darkness, blocking out the stars as it drew near, but mercifully bringing the support team with it.

Having seen the chopper as well, Captain Ellsworth began guiding it in to the DZ with his SARBE surface-to-air rescue beacon. Unfortunately, any hopes he might have been harbouring that the guerrillas had disappeared from the lower slopes were brutally dashed when what sounded like a couple of heavy GPMGs roared into action and two streams of green tracer arced up into the sky towards the Wessex. The chopper kept coming, flying between the lines of tracer, but just as it was approaching the hill, some of the tracer hit it, causing showers of sparks to burst from it and making it shudder and list dangerously.

Immediately, the captain and Dead-eye fired savage bursts from their SLRs, hoping to silence the GPMGs down the hill. They were supported by the roaring of Taff's Bren gun and the SLRs of Jimbo and the wounded Ben – but to no avail. The guerrillas returned the fire with a small-arms fusillade, causing bullets to dance off the sangar wall in showers of sparks that acted as beacons to the enemy marksmen.

Simultaneously, the lines of green tracer from the guerrillas' GPMGs converged on the helicopter, turning it into a giant sparkler, making it shudder again and list more heavily, now pouring smoke. Even as the chopper turned away, the pilot was informing Captain Ellsworth over the radio that it was badly damaged and had to return to base while it could still fly. There was no chance of landing the replacements. Over and out.

Though exasperated and disappointed, the SAS

men in both sangars gave the Wessex covering fire until it had limped out of sight, leaving a trail of smoke behind it. When it had disappeared in the dark sky, the men stopped firing, conserving the last of their precious ammunition, and Captain Ellsworth contacted Lieutenant-Colonel Callaghan at Thumier on the encoded A41.

'I'm afraid the Wessex didn't make it through,' he explained. 'It's damaged but luckily still flying, and limping back to base right now.'

'Yes,' Callaghan replied. 'We've been informed. What options are left to you?'

'None,' Ellsworth said bluntly. 'We'll have to make a run for it under cover of darkness.'

'Within range of the enemy?'

'Yes, boss.'

'Any other problems?'

'Two men wounded in the leg; one with a serious stomach complaint and fever – now unconscious.'

'Christ,' Callaghan said softly. After a brief pause, he asked: 'Can the wounded men walk?'

'Not too well, but they can manage.'

'They'll slow you down.'

'We all know that.'

'And the unconscious man?'

'We'll have to carry him on a makeshift stretch-er.'

'That means your hands are full.'

Ellsworth actually chuckled. 'Yes, boss.'

'Two leg wounds and an unconscious body. It sounds suicidal.'

'We don't have any option.'

There was a moment's uneasy silence, broken only by the static coming over the radio. The guerrillas, too, were silent, though probably still inching up the dark hill, determined to annihilate the Englishmen.

'What's the time of departure?' Callaghan asked eventually.

'Approximately 1930 hours.'

'Can you make that precisely?'

'Yes.'

'Good. We'll lay down an artillery barrage on the southern hill at 1932 sharp, covering the area between the sangars and the hamlet below it. When you exit the sangars at 1930, take the northern slope. You should be out of the sangars by the time the first shells of the barrage strike the southern hill. With luck, we can keep them engaged long enough for you to get out of range. They'll follow you, but at least you'll have a head start and a fighting chance.'

'We'll be out and gone, boss.'

'Right,' Callaghan replied. 'Good luck to all of you.'

Handing the radio back to Les, Captain Ellsworth said, 'That's it, men. We move out at 1930 sharp. That gives us approximately thirty minutes to pack up our kit.'

'We'll have to travel light,' Dead-eye said, 'so I recommend we leave anything we don't really need or can't reasonably carry.'

'Agreed. But don't leave it for the guerrillas. Destroy anything that might be of use to them.'

'Will do.'

'Right, lads, let's get to it. Dead-eye, can you crawl over to the other sangar and tell them what's happening?'

'Yes, boss.'

Dead-eye left the sangar and did the leopard crawl to the other sangar: wriggling forward on his belly, using his elbows for leverage, with his SLR cradled in both hands. While he was gone, the men he had left behind began to remove what kit they needed from their bergens, strap on their webbing and destroy any equipment they did not intend carrying. Even the A41 was smashed to pieces. The separate Morse set was rendered unusable by extracting the crystals that controlled its operating frequencies; then the men smashed what they could of the set itself. Even before Dead-eye had returned, the sounds of similar destruction could be heard coming from the smaller sangar. By the time he had crawled back into the larger sangar, all the work had been completed and the men, each carrying only his SLR, water bottle, ammunition pouches and emergency rations, were ready to move. All except the still-unconscious Terry.

'We'll have to make a stretcher,' Captain Ellsworth said.

'Right,' Dead-eye agreed. 'By hook or by crook, we've got to carry him out of here. For that reason, the men in the other sangar have agreed to give us covering fire for two minutes, only moving out when the artillery barrage begins.'

'Dangerous,' Ken murmured.

'Good of them to do it,' the captain said. 'Damned decent of them.'

Dead-eye checked his wristwatch. 'Our time's nearly up, boss. Let's get that stretcher made for Terry.'

Before anyone could move, however, the guerrillas, now much higher up the hill and inevitably hearing the noise from the smaller sangar, aimed a sustained fusillade of rifle and machine-gun fire at it. The men in the sangar immediately replied in kind and soon the green tracer of the guerrillas and the blue of the SAS were criss-crossing. Bullets bounced off the sangar and the rocks well below it, sending up showers of sparks.

'Fucking Guy Fawkes Night,' Ken murmured, rising painfully to the crouching position, head bowed to avoid the overhanging ponchos, his SLR in his hand.

Without a word, Dead-eye reached up and tore off the poncho, letting air rush in and revealing the stars directly above. He then removed some of the thicker branches holding the poncho up, checked their strength, then lay them parallel along both ends of the poncho and folded its ends over each stick. With his Sykes-Fairburn commando dagger, he stabbed holes in the turned-over ends and through the poncho below, along the whole length of both covered sticks. Removing a coil of heavy-duty string from his bergen, he cut it into two equal lengths and used the separate pieces to 'stitch' the folded-over ends of the poncho around the thick branches, thus completing a crude but effective stretcher.

He did all of this in about five minutes while Ken and Les, both kneeling by the wall and obviously in agony from their wounded legs, added their SLR fire to the combined Bren-gun and SLR fire from the smaller sangar.

'All right, boss,' Dead-eye said to Captain Ellsworth, 'let's put him onto this stretcher.'

Still kneeling and keeping their heads under the top of the sangar wall, they lifted the shivering, moaning trooper and deposited him awkwardly onto the makeshift stretcher. Dead-eye picked up Terry's SLR and slung it over his own shoulder.

'No point leaving it for the guerrillas,' he explained. 'And it might come in handy.'

Ellsworth checked his wristwatch, then raised his eyes again. 'One minute to go.' He turned to Ken and Les, who had both stopped firing to reload. 'Do you think you can make it on those legs?'

'I've been legless before,' Les said with a grin, 'and I always got home.'

'Same here,' Ken said.

Ellsworth grinned. 'Right. Here's the drill.' He glanced at his wristwatch again. 'When Dead-eye and I hump out with the stretcher, you two exit with us, one at the front, one behind. You give covering fire as all of us move down the northern slope. As we make our escape, we'll also be given covering fire by the other sangar. When we're 100 yards or so down the hill, we'll hit the ground and give covering fire to the men in the other sangar. When they reach us, we all take off together. By that time Callaghan's artillery barrage will have started. That'll put a wall of fire between us and the guerrillas, and give us a fighting chance. Any last-minute questions?'

Ken and Les shook their heads simultaneously.

'Good. Let's get ready.'

The stretcher lay parallel to the front of the sangar, one end pointing towards the gap in the side. Dead-eye knelt in front of the stretcher, between it and the exit, with his back turned to it. He had Terry's SLR slung over one shoulder, his own over the other. His hands were angled backwards to take hold of the ends of the two branches, acting as handles. Ellsworth did the same at the other end, but facing the stretcher. Ken and Les were crouching low, one on each side of the exit, both tormented by the pains shooting through their wounded legs, but both prepared to move out with Dead-eye and Ellsworth. The latter checked his wristwatch. One minute to go. He raised his right hand, preparing to give the signal for 'Go!'.

Suddenly, unexpectedly, a machine-gun roared from lower down the slope. Even before Ellsworth could drop his hand, a great chunk of stone was punched out of the lower part of the sangar's front wall and phosphorescent-green tracer shot through the space like a laser beam, before smashing through the back wall.

The stretcher appeared to explode beneath Terry, with pieces of branch and tattered strips of poncho flying everywhere as he was chopped to pieces by the vicious stream of tracer.

The sick trooper started screaming. He was jerking epileptically as the tracer bullets tore through both him and the stretcher, then passed above them and through the stones in the opposite wall. Some of the bullets flew around the sangar, expiring with a harsh, metallic clatter that only added to the deafening noise.

As abruptly as it had started firing, the machine-gun fell silent. Terry stopped screaming and his spasms subsided into the frozen, anguished posture of violent death. Looking down through the dust settling eerily over him, the shocked survivors in the sangar saw that he had been cut to pieces and now lay, lifeless and soaked in blood, on the smashed, tattered remains of the improvised stretcher.

'Not much we can do for him now,' Dead-eye said eventually, tonelessly. 'I think it's time we left, boss.'

Ellsworth glanced at Terry, then at his own wristwatch. He then raised and lowered his right hand.

'Go!' he screamed.

With a last look at the dead trooper, the four men ran at the crouch from the sangar. Outside, all hell broke loose.

13

As the four men burst out of the sangar to clatter noisily towards the northern slope, two of them wobbling uncertainly on wounded legs, the guerrillas either heard them or saw them silhouetted against the skyline and responded with a clamorous barrage of small-arms fire, most of it coming from behind a couple of large boulders surprisingly close to the two sangars.

Les, in the lead, fired back with his SLR as enemy bullets whistled past his head. Coming up right behind him, Dead-eye was also blasting away at the hostile rocks with the SLR at his hip. Captain Ellsworth was between the two, while Ken, unsteady on his wounded leg, was acting as back marker and managed to get off a burst or two.

'Keep going!' Ellsworth bawled. 'Don't stop! Head for the slope!'

More enemy bullets whipped and hissed about them as, up at the front, Les lurched forward as fast as his injured leg permitted, gritting his teeth against the pains that were stabbing up it with each step. Bringing up the rear, and firing his SLR on the move, Ken was suffering similar agony.

'Stop firing and move faster!' Dead-eye bawled.

'I can't!' Les protested.

In fact, he paused and turned to see if the others were still with him. As he did so, a machine-gun roared into action, adding its noise to the one giving cover from the smaller sangar, and green tracer arced out of the guerrilla positions, zipped between the running men, then moved left to cut across Captain Ellsworth, who shuddered violently, as if being electrocuted. Punched sideways, he was then spun around and hurled violently to the ground, hitting a small rock with a sickening thud and flopping onto his spine.

'Shit!' Dead-eye turned back while waving the other two onward, but they ignored him and stood their ground, giving him covering fire, as he ran up to Ellsworth and knelt beside him to examine him. He was badly mangled and clearly dead.

After stripping Ellsworth of his weapon and ammunition, Dead-eye ran back to the others at the crouch. Even as they were making their escape over the rim of the northern hill, the enemy machine-gunner and others using small arms were concentrating on Ellsworth. The combined force of their bullets jerked his body sideways across the slope until it was stopped by a rock. There it quivered constantly under the impact of more bullets and gradually turned into what looked like a tattered pile of rags.

That, at least, is all Dead-eye and the others saw the guerrillas picking up and carrying triumphantly off as their comrades spread out and advanced on the two sangars.

Deeply shocked by the loss of Captain Ellsworth, the other three men slipped over the rim of the southern hill, some 15 yards from the sangars, then lay belly down on the ground to give covering fire to Jimbo and his men.

Dead-eye groaned softly. 'Those guerrillas are practically on top of the sangar. Jimbo and the others haven't got a chance. They'll never get out of there.'

At that moment a deep thunder swelled up from far behind him and lightning illuminated the distant horizon. Within seconds the first shells from the 25-pounders in Thumier were ploughing into the southern hill, erupting in a series of fearsome explosions that tore up the soil, sand, gravel and rocks around and between the screaming guerrillas. Many Arabs were picked up and smashed back down in this lethal maelstrom.

Les whooped with joy. Ken just grinned at him. Even the inscrutable Dead-eye gave a slight grin; he had forgotten the promised barrage and was relieved to see it.

While the barrage was devastating the hill running down to the hamlet, turning it into a gigantic convulsion of swirling soil and gravel, and mushrooming smoke that obscured the screaming, spinning Arabs, the four survivors from the sangar – the original covering party of Jimbo, Larry, Ben and Taff – burst out into the night and headed rapidly down the north hill to join Dead-eye, Ken and Les.

In the event, they did not need covering fire as the guerrillas were so devastated by the barrage from the distant 25-pounders that they failed to notice the departure of the men from the smaller sangar.

'Where's the Bren?' Dead-eye asked.

'Shot to pieces,' Jimbo replied tersely. 'Not worth bringing out.'

Approaching that sangar in the darkness, out of the hell of explosions erupting further down the hill, the guerrillas opened fire with everything they had. When their bullets struck showers of silver sparks from the sangar walls, the guerrillas mistook them for the return fire of the SAS and decided to charge the position from both directions.

As the SAS men hurried away at the crouch, disappearing into the darkness, the guerrillas broke into two groups, encircled the smaller sangar, and fired on it from both directions. With neither group knowing which way the other had gone, each mistook the other's fire for the return fire of the SAS. They were mowing each other down in a bloody fire-fight.

'Beautiful!' Dead-eye murmured with satisfaction.

Using a pair of binoculars and his PNGs, he observed the activity of the Arabs. The artillery barrage on the lower slope had temporarily stopped when the guerrillas entered the smaller sangar and emerged empty-handed, barking angrily at one another. They then went into the larger sangar and emerged with Terry's lacerated body. As a couple of them carried him clumsily down the hill, another couple picked up the dead Captain Ellsworth and then followed them.

No sooner had they disappeared into the darkness of the southern slope than more shells from the big guns fell on the hill, but this time higher up, blowing the sangars to smithereens and gradually rearranging the topography of the hill with awesome efficiency.

When the barrage had ceased and the smoke had cleared away, no trace of the sangars was left and the top of the hill was pock-marked with enormous shell holes and covered with huge mounds of upturned, smouldering sand and soil.

'The bastards got the bodies of Captain Ellsworth and Terry,' Dead-eye said, lowering his binoculars and removing the PNGs to look steadily and unemotionally at the others. Then, before they could give in to shock, he said: 'Come on, let's get moving.'

Turning away from that still smoking scene of terrible devastation, they hurried all the way down the north hill, then out across the dried-up Wadi Rabwa, heading back towards the Dhala Road and Thumier. But they still had a long way to go.

14

Deeply shocked by their losses – the more so because the bodies had been carried off by the enemy – and suffering from psychological and physical fatigue, the men marched through what seemed like a nightmarish lunar landscape in a gloom that could not be relieved by humour. Dead-eye and Jimbo led the way, with Larry right behind them, still carrying his medical box on his shoulder. Taff and Ben followed Larry, while Ken and Les hobbled along painfully in the rear.

Ben's tunic had been slashed open by the bullet that had scorched across his back, and a bloody bandage showed through the tattered, flapping cloth. Les was limping very badly on his wounded leg, though losing no blood and clearly determined to make it back. But Ken was suffering much more, gradually slowing down, and stopping frequently to adjust the bandage around his thigh, from which blood was still seeping at a dangerous rate.

They were marching along the crest of the hill, heading south-west, parallel to the wadi far below, whose darkness was broken by striations of silver moonlight. Even at night it was warm, with a clammy breeze, and all of them were soon pouring sweat and feeling parched.

After Ken had stopped for the third or fourth time to adjust his bandage, Larry glanced back, saw the seeping blood and hurried to him.

'Jesus,' Larry said, 'why didn't you tell me?'

'I didn't want to hold us up.'

'You'll hold us up more if I don't treat that. Take a seat, soldier.'

With one hand, Larry indicated to Dead-eye and Jimbo that they had to stop for a while; with the other he gently pushed the wincing corporal down onto the stony earth. Kneeling beside him, he removed the original, blood-soaked bandage, cleaned the two bullet holes with antiseptic and applied fresh dressings.

'I wish I could take those bullets out,' he said, 'but I can't risk it here. I've already lost one man; I don't want to lose you.'

'You didn't lose Terry,' Ken told him. 'He was shot to pieces.'

'Which he might not have been had I treated him and kept him off that stretcher. I should have done more for him.'

'You're a medic, not a doctor, for Christ's sake. You did all you could for him.'

'I still feel bad.'

'We all do – for him and for Ellsworth.'

'Yes, a good officer.'

'One of the best.'

Completing the dressing of the wound, Larry patted Ken on the shoulder, then moved across to Les, who was gingerly examining the bloody bandage around his own wounded leg. The bandages were soaked in caked blood to which dust and sand had stuck.

'At least the bleeding's stopped,' Larry said as he cut away the four old dressings that Les had applied himself and which were now flapping loose.

'Yeah,' Les replied with a tight grin. 'That's a blessing, I suppose.'

'Does it hurt?'

'Only when I put my foot on the ground.'

'Which you'll have to do a lot,' Larry said.

'Don't remind me, Sawbones.'

Smiling reassuringly, Larry removed the last of the old bandages, cleaned and checked the wound – it was not too bad, though not helpful for marching – then applied antiseptic and redressed it. He then went over to have a look at Ben, who was at that very moment wincing and arching his wounded back.

'Does it hurt?' Larry asked, kneeling beside Ben, close to Taff.

'What the fuck do *you* think?' Ben replied in his pugnacious manner.

'It's only a scratch,' Taff said with a sly grin. 'Anyone'd think he'd been hurt really badly!'

'Fuck you, Taff,' Ben shot back. 'That bullet gouged out a length of skin and bloody near killed me to boot. I don't see *you* being so brave about it.'

Taff pointed to Ken and Les. 'Those two have *real* wounds,' he said, trying to keep his spirits up by taking a rise out of Ben. 'Not a poxy little scratch across the back.' He turned to Larry. 'His wound doesn't hurt,' he explained. 'It just stings a bit.'

'Go fuck yourself,' Ben said.

When Larry parted the torn tunic, he saw that

there was indeed a combination of gouged skin and a burn mark running in a diagonal line across Ben's back. After getting the trooper to remove the tunic, he examined the wound more thoroughly and saw that the gouge was deep, almost cutting through to the bone, and that the burning effects of the hot bullet had actually congealed the blood, thus doing some good.

Ben, he realized, was not exaggerating when he said that the bullet had nearly killed him. In fact, if he had moved just a fraction backwards, the bullet would have entered through his waist and shot up through his chest at the same angle, shredding everything in its path, before possibly emerging from just under his armpit and then ploughing through his shoulder, which it would have smashed to pieces on its way out. In the event, it had merely left a deep, burnt furrow in the skin, running obliquely across Ben's back from the left side of his spine to the right shoulder. Almost certainly it did more than merely sting; it probably hurt like hell.

'Very nice,' Larry said. 'Really quite artistic. I'm going to apply some cream which will hurt at first, but then gradually act as an anaesthetic. The wound won't sting after the cream takes effect.'

'It's more than a *sting*!' Ben insisted.

'Ha, ha,' Taff cackled.

Ben winced as Larry applied the cream. But he relaxed completely when the wound was covered in cream and already starting to hurt less. Larry then wrapped a lengthy bandage repeatedly around Ben's torso, until most of his back had been covered. When he had finished tying the knot, he stood up and told Ben to put his tunic back on.

'You can close that long tear with safety pins,' he advised him. 'That'll keep the breeze off it.'

'The breeze is warm,' Ben said.

'It'll blow sand over the dressing and some of it could work its way under it and into the wound. Close up that tear, Trooper.'

'Yes, Sawbones,' Ben said, removing some small safety pins from his escape and survival belt and proceeding to pin up the tear in his tunic.

'Feeling better, then?' Taff asked innocently.

'Yeah,' Ben said, speaking with the safety pins in his mouth and clipping one over the tear in his tunic.

'You just needed a little attention,' Taff said. 'All mummy's boys do.'

'Up yours,' Ben grunted.

Returning to the front of the file, Larry was approached by Dead-eye and Jimbo.

'How are they?' the latter asked.

'Trooper Riley's all right – his wound's only superficial. Lance-Corporal Moody's gonna have a painful march, but I think he can make it.'

'And Corporal Brooke?' Dead-eye asked.

'His leg wound's pretty bad. I can't stop the bleeding. He needs a proper surgical operation and I can't give him that. The more he marches, the more he's going to bleed. I don't know how long he can go like that, but the sooner we get back the better.'

'But he *can* march?' Jimbo asked anxiously.

'He'll be slow, but he can march.'

'OK,' Dead-eye said, 'let's march.' He raised his right hand, then let it drop, indicating 'Forward march'.

The men climbed laboriously to their feet and began their long trek south-west, struggling up and down the steep, irregular walls of parched water channels that had once fed the wadi below. The network of gullies criss-crossing the rocky slope did not make the going any easier – and in fact made it hell for the two men with leg wounds – while the walls, even steeper than the hill, were encrusted with sharp stones.

As the march continued and the moon rose

higher, spilling more light on the wadi and the desert plain beyond it, Les limped gamely on, muttering curses each time his leg hurt. Ken, however, was suffering even more, for both his wounds were being opened by the constant strain of the climbs and bleeding even worse than before. Forced to stop twice to let Larry attend to him, he was noticeably white and strained-looking, breathing heavily and undoubtedly weakening. Nevertheless, when his wounds had been attended to, the march had to go on.

'We should have made a stretcher for Corporal Brooke,' Jimbo whispered to Dead-eye when both of them were marching up at the front, on point. 'We need one right now.'

'There was only enough wood for one stretcher,' Dead-eye informed him, 'and the one we got out of it was shot to hell.'

Jimbo glanced left and right at the barren, moonlit hill and the flat desert plain beyond it. 'Nothing here, I suppose.'

'No, Jimbo, nothing. No wood. No poncho sheets.'

Jimbo glanced back over his shoulder at the limping Les and then at Ken, desperately struggling along. 'He's not going to make it,' he said quietly.

'He's got to. Those guerrillas will be on our tail, so we have to keep moving.'

They marched for another hour – until clouds passed over the moon and blocked out most of the light. Then the march became even more difficult because they had to climb in and out of the pitch-black gullies without the benefit of light. At the same time an insidious combination of shock and exhaustion was attacking their nervous systems and making them tense, irritable and – even more dangerous – highly imaginative. They heard the enemy in every unfamiliar sound, and saw him in the shifting of the sands, the rustling of clumps of aloe and euphorbia, the shivering of jujube trees.

They marched over high sand dunes, back down into dark gullies, across stretches of dangerously smooth volcanic rock, staying parallel to the wadi, which would lead them eventually to the Dhala Road. At one point the moon passed between two banks of clouds, briefly shedding its light across the level strip ahead, before plunging it back into near total darkness.

In that brief illumination Jimbo thought he saw a group of Arab tents. He and Dead-eye dropped immediately to the ground, with the men behind

229

them following suit. By the time they were belly down in the sand, the clouds had covered the moon again and the remaining light was of little use. When Jimbo's eyes got used to the darkness, he saw the tents again.

'Arab tents,' he whispered to Dead-eye.

'You think so?'

'For sure.'

'They're certainly shaped like tents,' Dead-eye said, 'but they're very still.'

'Naturally,' Jimbo said. 'Most of the bastards are asleep. The camp will be guarded, though. What should we do? Fight it out, sneak around them, or what?'

Dead-eye tried using his binoculars and PNGs, but even in the green glow of the night vision goggles the tents were relatively indistinct and could not be seen clearly. He did, however, see to the left of the tents what could either have been shivering trees or restless camels. Though doubting his own senses, not sure that what he was looking at was actually an Arab camp, he said: 'With Brooke and Moody in the shape they're in, we can't take any chances. So let's climb higher, circle above them, and maybe we'll see more clearly as we pass over them.'

'Right,' Jimbo said.

Giving the 'Follow me' hand signal, Dead-eye and Jimbo led the others further up the hill in a circular direction that gradually brought them directly above the problem. Looking down, they realized that the tents had been pitched directly above the main wadi and the track they had been looking for themselves.

Cursing under his breath, Dead-eye indicated that the others should lie belly down behind him. He did the same, then studied the tents through his binoculars and his PNGs.

'Rocks,' he said, passing the binoculars and PNGs to Jimbo. 'Rocks and shivering doum palms.' When the latter had also studied the 'tents', he handed back the binoculars and PNGs with a rueful grin. 'You win,' he said.

'Still,' Dead-eye replied, 'we found the track we've been looking for, so let's get ourselves down there.'

To descend they had to march farther around the hill, almost completing their broad arc, until they came to a goat track that wound down in the right direction. It was very steep, and sliding gravel and sand made it difficult for most of the men to keep their balance. If it was hard for them, it was close to hell for the wounded Ken and Les, both of whom were visibly twitching from the pains shooting through their legs and lagging behind with increasing frequency.

Finally, when Dead-eye saw that Ken had fallen behind and this time was making no attempt to catch up, he started back down the line. Ken saw him coming, waved frantically, silently, for him to stay out of sight, then lowered himself to the ground, gingerly holding his leg.

Dead-eye and the others instantly hit the ground, then Dead-eye advanced by the leopard crawl until he reached Ken. The corporal pointed back the way they had come.

'Someone's following us,' he mouthed as if speaking to a deaf person, not wanting to be heard by the guerrillas.

When Dead-eye wrinkled his forehead in a questioning manner, Ken nodded and again pointed back along the track, to where it curved around some rocks and disappeared in the darkness.

Raising his left hand – the other was gripping his SLR – Dead-eye spread his fingers, then dropped them one by one, asking silently how many guerrillas Ken thought he had seen. Ken raised a single finger of his left hand, then three of his right, indicating that one man was in the lead, followed by three others.

Dead-eye glanced at the corporal's leg and saw that again blood was seeping through the soaked bandages and dripping to the ground. Raising his eyes, he carefully studied Ken's face and saw that it was deathly white, the skin drawn taut on the cheekbones, betraying great physical and mental stress. The corporal was clearly in considerable pain and losing strength through loss of blood. Was he hallucinating?

Dead-eye was just about to don his PNGs and unclip his binoculars when he heard a noise from along the trail and looked back to where it curved out of sight around the tall rocks. An Arab in an off-white jellaba appeared around the rock, treading carefully and carrying a .303 Lee-Enfield. His fluttering *shemagh* was covering his mouth and nose, making him look like a bandit.

Dead-eye rolled instantly to one side of the track, indicating that Ken should go to the opposite side. Unable to move so quickly and not willing to roll on his wounded leg, Ken gritted his teeth, then forced himself up into a crouching position and made his way to the other side of the track. Once there, he lay down on his belly behind some thorn bushes, taking aim along the Trilux sight of his SLR. On his own side of the track, Dead-eye did the same.

Glancing back where he had come from, he was relieved to see that the rest of the patrol had disappeared from the track and had doubtless divided up to hide at both sides of it. Glancing to the front, he saw that the Arab scout was drawing ever closer and that three others were just appearing around the tall boulder.

Looking across the track, he saw Ken staring at him, waiting for some kind of instruction. Using his index finger, Dead-eye pointed first to Ken, then to the Arab in the lead, indicating that the corporal was to concentrate on him. When Ken nodded that he understood, Dead-eye pointed to the three men behind, jabbing his finger three times, indicating that he was going to deal with them while Ken was to shoot the scout. Again Ken nodded.

Still belly down on the ground, Dead-eye released the safety-catch on his SLR and carefully took aim. Only the quiet tread of the Arabs' slippers broke what seemed like a very lengthy silence but was in fact no more than a few seconds.

Dead-eye waited until the scout was only ten yards away, then fired the first shot at one of the three men behind him. Even before the guerrilla had staggered back from the impact of the bullet, Ken was firing his own first shot, which punched the scout backwards, then made him twist to the side, dropping his weapon and falling face down. He had yet to hit the ground when Dead-eye fired at the second of the three men behind him.

The sound of his shot was followed almost instantly by Ken's second, both bullets hitting the same man. As this unfortunate was jerking convulsively from the double impact and dropping his weapon, before falling himself, the final man dived desperately for the shelter of the tall rock just behind him.

Dead-eye and Ken fired at the same instant. The latter missed his moving target, but the former put a bullet into the Arab's side, spinning him over and throwing him to the ground with his rifle clattering noisily away from him. Surprisingly, he clambered to his knees, clutching his blood-soaked jellaba, then scrambled forward to get at his weapon.

Again, Dead-eye and Ken fired simultaneously, this time both hitting the target. The Arab was punched left, then right; then he slammed backwards into the rock, his skull cracking as he did so. Sliding slowly along it, he dropped to his knees, then flopped forward into the dust, where he quivered like a bowstring for a few seconds, then collapsed and was still.

None of the guerrillas made a sound. That meant there were no wounded. Even so, Dead-eye climbed carefully to his feet and walked over to the scout. Kicking him gently and receiving no response, he moved on to the other three men and confirmed that all of them were dead.

Relieved, but still wary, he walked to the bend in the track, switched the SLR to automatic, and fired a lengthy burst into the darkness, thereby hoping to dissuade any other guerrillas lurking there from following immediately. When he heard nothing and saw nothing, he turned back the way he had come.

Ken was staring enquiringly at him, his face gleaming with sweat, the skin taut with strain. Dead-eye nodded, indicating that the job was done. He walked up to the corporal and said: 'You didn't do badly for a wounded man. How's the leg?'

'Terrible.' Ken sat down gently in the dirt, his legs stretched out in front of him. He wiped sweat from his face and tentatively exercised his wounded leg. 'Christ!' he said softly.

One by one the rest of the SAS patrol emerged from behind bushes at both sides of the track and walked up to find out what had happened. When Jimbo saw the four dead Arabs on the track, he gave a low whistle and said: 'Not a trick of the moonlight this time!'

'No,' Dead-eye replied. 'They were following us . . . and they certainly wouldn't have come alone. The others can't be far behind.'

'You fired a burst along the track?'

'Yes.'

'No response?'

'No.'

'Still,' Jimbo said, 'I recommend we do a double check by setting up here in ambush positions for another ten minutes. If no one appears by then, we'll know they're a good way behind and we can move off again.'

'You men agree with that?' Dead-eye asked, as if conducting a 'Chinese parliament', taking in the opinions of the others, including the troopers. All of them nodded silently. 'All right, let's spread out.'

They divided into two groups and assumed ambush positions behind the thorn bushes at both sides of the track. They waited for another ten minutes, but there was no sound except the moaning of the warm wind blowing over the dead men. The dust covered them gradually.

15

Eventually, satisfied that the guerrillas were not close behind them, the SAS men moved off again. This time, however, they marched even more cautiously than before, each man glancing back from time to time, checking that no Arabs were in sight. For the first hour, at least, they saw no one and could march on in peace.

Out in front on point, Dead-eye trudged in grim silence along the track that would lead to the Dhala Road, across a flat stretch of desert, closely bordered on both sides by high ridges. Keeping his eyes peeled and never forgetting what he was doing, he was nevertheless dwelling bitterly on the deaths of Captain Ellsworth and Trooper Malkin.

Impelled by his life-long ambition to be a good soldier, and forged like steel in the hell of the

Telok Anson swamp in Malaya and the jungles of Borneo, Dead-eye usually accepted the death of comrades with equanimity, studiously avoiding any kind of sentimentality. This time, however, while not giving in to sentiment, he was burning up with bitterness, not just because of the loss of two good men but because their deaths had been unnecessary.

Proud to be in the SAS, Dead-eye normally believed in what he was fighting for, but such was not the case here in the Radfan. This was a politicians' war, a public relations campaign, and Dead-eye resented the fact that two worthy men had died for no good reason. He also felt humiliated because, as Callaghan had said, this was not a war that could be won and what had happened to this patrol was proof of that. They were retreating with their tails between their legs and, even more shameful, had left two dead SAS men in the hands of the enemy.

Marching behind Dead-eye, Jimbo was less bitter, though not exactly happy with his lot. Glancing across the flat, dark desert, then left and right at the high, potentially treacherous ridges, he was reminded of his earliest days with the SAS, in the North African desert. That had been a real war, an honourable war, vastly different to this mean little action in a place that few people back home knew existed. Even now, Jimbo could recall his adventures in North Africa only with pride and exhilaration: racing in on the enemy positions in the Chevrolet lorries of the Long Range Desert Group, the wind in your face, machine-guns roaring from the back of the open vehicles, then speeding out again before the enemy knew what had hit them. It had been a war fought by men who believed in what they were doing and were proud to be doing it.

Jimbo was particularly proud of having fought with the original founder of the Regiment, Captain David Stirling, as well as Lieutenant-Colonel Callaghan, his present CO at HQ Thumier and a bit of a regimental legend in his own right. He remembered with fondness, too, the other ranks he had known and respected, many since dead in Malaya or Borneo. That pride in those he had fought with, the fights he had fought and the Regiment in general was something he did not feel now as the patrol made its way along the wind-blown desert track towards the Dhala Road. This was virtually a 'secret' war, unknown to most people. It was secret because it was dirty and fought for no good reason against an enemy that did not respect you and for whom you had no respect. Jimbo could not stomach that.

Marching between Jimbo and Larry, Ben and Taff had no feelings about this war one way or the other, having nothing to compare it with. Being new to the Regiment and on their first mission with it, both of them were in a state of shock over the deaths of Captain Ellsworth and Terry, which, in some unvoiced way, they had not quite expected. They were further depressed by the fact that Ken and Les, the two soldiers from whom they had hoped to learn the most, as they were their direct superiors, were in fact badly wounded and, in Ken's case, starting to show distinct signs of stress.

When they glanced back over their shoulders, as they felt compelled to do often, they saw, well behind Larry, the two back markers, Ken and Les, hobbling along side by side, the latter desperately coaxing his mate onward. Ken was in a bad way, bleeding profusely, and his consequent loss of strength was making him lose control and behave like a crazy man. Les was in better shape, though clearly suffering. Neither man was any longer in a position to help the two troopers.

Ben and Taff felt isolated, more dependent upon one another. They respected Jimbo and were in awe of Dead-eye, but neither NCO was as approachable as Ken or Les had been before they were wounded. Everything had changed, and the two troopers were now besieged by doubts.

Their uncertainty was exaggerated by their mounting physical and mental exhaustion, but they were not experienced enough to know that. Having been badged together, flown to Aden together, thrown up in the trucks together and shared their baptism of fire together, they felt very close, almost like brothers, taking strength from one another in order to combat the rigours of this hellish hike through the dangerous night.

Larry was fighting his fatigue and delayed shock by thinking of his girlfriend, Cathy, and wondering what she was doing right now, back in Devon. Formerly of the Royal Army Medical Corps (RAMC) and having previously served with the SAS in Borneo, Larry was a good, experienced soldier who had witnessed violent death before and suffered the horrors of swamp and jungle. This had not hardened his heart to such a degree that he could, like Dead-eye, bury his feelings about lost comrades. Nor could it make him view romance as something trivial when compared with war's brutal realities. So, while Larry suffered silently like the others, shocked by the two deaths, disturbed by the wounding of the other men, and increasingly twitchy from lack of sleep and exhaustion, he was able to endure it by conjuring up visions of the girl he loved.

He did this, however, while maintaining a good degree of vigilance: on the one hand constantly checking for any sign of enemy movement behind the rocks on the ridges on both sides of the desert track; on the other, occasionally letting himself fall back to where Ken and Les were acting as back markers more by will-power than anything else.

No matter how many times Larry came back down the line to bandage Ken's bloody left thigh, the two bullet holes kept bleeding, relentlessly draining Ken of physical strength and, inevitably, weakening him mentally as well. It was now clear to Larry, as it was to the others, that not only was Ken in serious danger from loss of blood, but he was starting to ramble in thought and action. He jumped at every unfamiliar sound, saw the enemy in every shadow, and had started mumbling constantly to himself in his growing delirium.

Designated as back markers because they were

the slowest and always falling behind anyway, the two wounded men were as mutually supportive as they could be in the circumstances. Les had taken it upon himself to be Ken's crutch. Ken was his friend and a hell of a good soldier, but he was now in a terrible mess.

Hardened by his experiences with the 3rd Battalion, Royal Green Jackets, in Malaya and Borneo, Les was willing and able to endure the screaming agony in his own wounded leg each time he placed his right foot on the ground, which was every second or so for the past two hellish hours. But even he was finding it difficult to endure his own pain while attending to his friend, who kept stopping and starting, and seemed anxious to wander out of the file and head for one or other of the ridges on either side of the desert track. While trying to maintain his own equilibrium by visualizing a foaming pint in his local in Southend, or placing a winning bet, or making love either to his wife or some bint he had picked up in a pub, Les attempted to keep his friend occupied by talking constantly to him about his wife and three children back home in Somerset, the joys of wildlife photography in the Brendon Hills, which Ken had done so often, and the prospect of once again fishing and hiking on

Exmoor. Ken responded coherently at times, but mostly with incomprehension, mumbling about being too warm and having a dry throat.

Unfortunately, the minute Les stopped talking to him, Ken would focus his increasingly unhinged mind on the ridges to left and right, often starting at some imagined sound or movement, raising his weapon, intending to fire it, but always prevented from doing so by Les. He stopped, he started, he slumped down again, severely hampering the progress of the patrol.

Given Ken's penchant for seeing enemies in every shifting shadow and unfamiliar sound, it came as a surprise to Les when he himself thought he had heard movement behind him and turned around to check if someone was following. He did this more than once and never saw anyone, but each time he heard the sound it seemed closer, until eventually it sounded like the rustle of slippered feet.

As the track curved back around the eastern ridge, where it disappeared into darkness, Les could not see very far. Yet when again he stopped and strained to hear, he was convinced he was listening to the sound of more than one man advancing and hurrying to catch up. He was not mistaken.

Ken was just about to wander off the track yet again when Les grabbed him by the shoulder and pulled him down with him to the ground. Turning onto his side, he then used a hand signal to indicate to Larry that someone was following them. The same hand signal then went from man to man along the line until it reached Dead-eye, still out on point. At another hand signal from Dead-eye, the men gathered together, then split into two firing groups, one to each side of the track, as before. Hidden behind parched jujube and doum palms, the men adopted kneeling positions, then cocked their SLRs and aimed them at the trail on a point of impact some 15 yards away.

Ken, Les noticed, was alert enough to have done the same, though his wounded leg, propping him up in the kneeling position, was visibly shaking and seeping blood.

Though the wait seemed interminable, it was less than two minutes. Eventually, the men on their trail emerged stealthily from the darkness, both wearing jellabas and *shemaghs*, and carrying .303 Lee-Enfields. One was looking down to check the footprints on the trail, the other carefully scanning the track ahead. The latter was obviously also scanning both sides of the road, but could not see the SAS men in the distance. Satisfied that they were still well ahead, he nodded to his companion and both men advanced along the track.

The SAS men aimed along their Trilux sights. The signal to fire would be the sound of Dead-eye's first shot. He waited until the guerrillas were at the estimated point of impact for most of the weapons, then he fired at the man nearest to him.

The other SLRs roared simultaneously in a short, shocking fusillade that peppered the two Arabs with 7.62mm bullets, making them convulse wildly, drop their weapons, stagger first left, then right, and finally fling themselves to opposite sides of the track as more bullets spat off rocks and stones, creating billowing, swirling clouds of dust around them. In fact, they were already dead, torn to shreds by the fusillade, but one man, at least, kept firing at them as if he could not stop.

Having switched to automatic and aiming from right to left, from one dead Arab to the other, Ken was continuing to fire as he clambered to his feet, wobbling on his wounded leg, muttering to himself and pumping one burst after another into the dead men. His bullets kicked up a hail of sand, soil, gravel and broken stones over the tattered bodies of the Arabs, jolting them first this way, then that, in an insane dance of death.

Ken kept firing until he ran out of ammunition. Then, in a demented fury, he once again began talking unintelligibly to himself as he frantically changed the twenty-round box magazine, wiped sweat from his white, drawn face, raised the weapon and took aim again.

Les ran up to him, slapped his hand over the plastic foregrip of the SLR, pushed the barrel down, then gently removed the weapon from his friend's hands. Ken stared at him, bewildered, then staggered to the side of the track to sit down and weep.

At a nod from Dead-eye, Larry hurried up to the grieving corporal, knelt beside him, whispered to him and gave him some tablets. Ken swallowed them without protest, then stretched out on his back and closed his wet eyes. He covered his face with his hands and took deep, even breaths.

There was an uneasy silence for what seemed like an eternity. Eventually rejoining the men after checking that the Arabs were dead, Jimbo glanced at Ken, then said to his fellow sergeant: 'It's two in the morning. We've been awake for 30 hours. We've been under pressure for most of

that time and I think it's enough. We need a break,
Dead-eye.'

'A break won't help Brooke.'

'It won't do him any harm. And the fitter we
are tomorrow, the more chance we have of getting
back. He can't be helped properly until we get
back, so that's our priority.'

'What's your suggestion?'

'We're now far enough away from Shi'b Taym
to drop back down towards the main Wadi Rabwa.
From there to the camp is only a mile or so.'

'I don't think those guerrillas are from Shi'b
Taym. I think they came from the ridge above.'

'So?'

'It doesn't matter that it's only a mile or so to
the camp. If the guerrillas have moved along that
ridge above us, we're gonna have a rough ride.
They'll keep sending men down throughout the
night and, if that fails, they'll start sniping at us
in the morning as we make our way back.'

Jimbo shrugged. 'What the fuck? We've no
choice. Assuming you're wrong and those guerrillas were from Shi'b Taym, I suggest that we
march on for another hour, but set an ambush
every fifteen minutes to see if anyone catches up.
If, after an hour, it's clear that I'm wrong and

you're right – that the guerrillas are up on the ridge – then we simply basha down for the night, get the rest we badly need, and take our chances on making it through at first light. At least then we'll feel a lot less tired and be more in control. What do you think?'

'Chinese parliament,' Dead-eye said. Turning to the others, he asked: 'So, what do *you* think? Those of you who agree, put up your hands.'

With the exception of Ken, still covering his face with his hands where he lay on his back, they all raised a hand.

Dead-eye nodded. 'All right, let's do it.' He glanced down at Ken. 'Corporal Brooke?' Ken removed his hands from his face and looked up with wet, red-rimmed eyes. 'Feel better now?' Ken just nodded. 'Can you march for another hour?' Ken nodded again. 'OK,' Dead-eye said, trying to sound as normal as possible. 'Climb to your feet and take your SLR off Moody.'

'Yes, Sarge,' Ken said. He pushed himself to his feet, dusted himself down, glanced uneasily at the two dead Arabs on the track, then took his SLR from Les. 'Thanks, mate,' he said.

'No problem,' Les replied.

'For everything,' Ken emphasized.

'*Still* no problem,' said Les.

Seeing that Ken, though obviously in a dreadful physical condition, had been pacified by the drugs given to him by Larry and was now more in control of himself, Dead-eye nodded at Jimbo, then, without a word, raised his right hand and waved the patrol forward. Falling instinctively into the same file formation as before – Dead-eye and Jimbo sharing point out front, followed by Ben and Taff, with Larry between them, and the two wounded men bringing up the rear as back markers – the men set off again, marching along the desert track that ran parallel to the main Wadi Rabwa.

Every fifteen minutes they stopped and divided into two firing groups, one to each side of the track. There they waited for ten minutes, listening for the sound of approaching footsteps. In the end, after half a dozen such stops in two and a half hours, during which time they covered no more than a mile, no guerrillas materialized and Dead-eye accepted that if they were still in danger, it would not come from the road behind them, but from the ridges above.

'So let's keep going,' he said, 'and get this over and done with.'

'No,' Jimbo said firmly. 'I don't think that's wise.

Apart from the fact that we still need to get some rest, regaining our alertness, we have to consider the possibility that if we approach the base camp in darkness we'll be fired upon by the FRA sentries at Thumier before we get the chance to identify ourselves. On both counts, then, I'd recommend bedding down now and moving on in daylight.'

Aware that Jimbo was a veteran of the SAS's earliest days with the LRDG in North Africa, and therefore bowing down respectfully to his greater experience, Dead-eye asked of the rest of the men: 'Is that all right with you?'

They all nodded.

'All right,' Dead-eye continued. 'Given what Jimbo's just said, I think the best way to avoid the FRA sentries tomorrow is to approach the camp by way of the wadi. The wadi will also offer us some protection from any guerrillas lurking up there on the ridges. So although I know you're exhausted, I'm asking you to take a deep breath and force yourselves to make that final hike back down into the wadi. Once there, we'll basha down for the night, then move out at first light. All agreed?'

There was no opposition to the plan. Dead-eye led the patrol in the same formation off the track, across a short stretch of desert, and back down the steep, rocky slope to the wide, dried-up wadi at the bottom. The descent was, as usual, hazardous, the men repeatedly slipping and sliding on loose gravel, tripping over stones, and becoming entangled in parched thorn bushes. But eventually, dazed with fatigue, they all made it down. Miraculously, they found a thin, babbling stream at the bottom of the hill.

'I don't believe it,' Dead-eye said.

'Wonders never cease,' Jimbo added.

Larry dipped his hand in the stream, then held it up high, letting the water drip off his fingers. 'It's real enough,' he announced.

'We were told not to drink from unpurified water,' Taff said, though he was licking his lips.

'He's right,' Ben said, wiping his lips with his hand.

Larry held his water bottle up high, shaking it to show that it was empty. Then he rapped his medical box with the knuckles of his free hand, saying, with a broad grin: 'I've got a bag full of sterilization tablets if there are any takers.'

'I'm in,' Jimbo said, and the rest all signalled their agreement with nods or raised hands.

'That's it, then,' Dead-eye said. 'We basha down

here for the night and move out in the morning. Let's get organized, men.'

As they were all close to dehydration, the first thing the men did was accept their quota of sterilization tablets from Larry. They dropped them into their empty water bottles, which they filled with water from the river, and then, when the tablets had dissolved, quenched their raging thirst. Slightly rejuvenated, they ate the last of the high-calorie rations from their escape and survival belts – chocolate, dry biscuits and cheese – then made themselves as comfortable as possible on the rough, sandy ground near the tinkling stream, in the shelter of overhanging rocks.

Seriously weakened by loss of blood, Ken sank into unconsciousness. The rest of the men, having slaked their thirst and filled their bellies, soon sank into a desperately needed sleep. Only Les, tormented by his inflamed leg, had trouble dropping off to sleep; though eventually he, too, received this simplest of blessings.

So exhausted were they that all of them slept through first light. Their communal peace was shattered soon after by gunfire.

16

Dead-eye was the first to get back on his feet, in the kneeling position behind his rock, as .303 bullets thudded into the ground between the other men, covering it with spouting, hissing sand. Looking up, he saw that they were being fired at by snipers who had taken up positions high on the eastern ridge and were silhouetted by the rising sun.

'Shit!' Dead-eye muttered, looking sideways to see that the other men were now taking up firing positions behind the rocks they had slept against. The guerrillas' bullets were still kicking up choking dust, dancing noisily off the rocks and hurling jagged pieces of stone at the SAS men. More bullets were hitting the tiny stream, creating small, crazily swirling fountains of water.

'Don't fire back!' Dead-eye bawled, aware that they would now need every last bullet.

Hiding behind a rock about ten feet away, Jimbo suddenly burst out from behind it and ran at the zigzag to Dead-eye, where he threw himself down, then scrambled into the kneeling position. After wiping sand from his face and glancing up at the ridge, where about forty silhouetted figures, all still firing, could clearly be seen, Jimbo spat at the ground.

'Fuck! We can't move!' he hissed.

'We've got to,' Dead-eye said.

'They'll chop us to pieces if we try. There's a lot of them up there.'

Dead-eye glanced at the other men and saw that they were all crouched behind separate rocks: Ben and Taff, both alert; Larry on his own, also alert; and Les whispering something to Ken, who, having regained consciousness during the night, was now squatting on the ground, looking dazed.

'Right,' Jimbo said, following Dead-eye's gaze, 'I can see what you see. Corporal Brooke's going to make the problem worse. We can't move fast with him.'

'Moody's looking after him.'

'Then Moody's going to get shot to pieces. It's goodbye and Amen.'

The shooting suddenly stopped, letting silence descend. Looking up at the ridge, Dead-eye saw that the guerrillas were moving back and forth, taking up better firing positions, now given the benefit of daylight. Most of them were spreading farther along the summit of the ridge, which offered them a broader arc of fire along the wadi, but some were slithering down the slope to get closer to their quarry.

'Hey, Sarge!' Ben called out as he watched the Arabs slithering downhill. 'Those bastards are sitting ducks up there. Let's pick a few off!'

'No!' Dead-eye shouted back. 'We're running short of ammo. We must save what we have until we really need it.'

'When's that?'

'I'll let you know, Trooper.'

The silence was eerie, broken only by the sound of running water and the occasional shout of one Arab calling out to the other.

'They're waiting for us to move out from behind these rocks,' Jimbo said. 'That's why they've stopped firing. The second we step out from cover, they'll start up again.'

Dead-eye studied the wadi that ran towards the Dhala Road and then on to Thumier. It was very wide, perhaps half a mile, and littered with boulders. Checking his map, he estimated that the Dhala Road was less than two miles away. The guerrillas would either have to come off the ridge and then engage in Close Quarters Battle or go back the way they had come.

'The question,' he said to Jimbo, 'is how far can we get in one piece if we move carefully from one rock to another. Can we get clear of the wadi?'

Jimbo checked the terrain, then scratched his nose and pursed his naturally twisted lips. 'It's possible,' he said. 'Not guaranteed, but possible. Given Corporal Brooke's condition, we're going to have to move anyway, so taking our time going from one rock to another won't make that much difference.'

They both studied the wadi again, mentally mapping out the best route to take.

'So what if we reach the end of the wadi?' Jimbo asked. 'Even if they retreat, we might still have the problem of being shot at by our own troops in Thumier.'

'I don't think so,' Dead-eye said. 'In fact, if the guerrillas follow us that far they might do us a favour. At the end of the wadi, we'll be close enough to Thumier for the FRA sentries to hear the sounds of battle. When they do, they'll know it's a fire-fight between us and the guerrillas and come out to support us. I think it's worth trying.'

'You've won my heart, darlin'.'

Dead-eye relayed the plan to the others by shouting at the top of his lungs. Everyone but Ken roared their agreement. Glancing across to where Ken was still squatting on the ground, he saw that he was slipping away, his head bowed, his chin resting on his chest.

'Is he unconscious?' Dead-eye shouted at Les.

When Les deliberately took hold of Ken's shoulder and shook him, the latter raised his head and glanced dazedly around him, blinking wildly.

'Can you get him along the wadi?' Jimbo asked.

'I can try,' Les shouted back. 'At least I'll stick with him all the way.'

'Good.' Dead-eye turned slightly aside to give instructions to the others. 'All right,' he bawled. 'Boulder to boulder, rock to rock. At the crouch, zigzagging. Don't try to get too far on any single run; make each run as short and as quick as possible. Conserve your ammunition. Only fire when giving cover to the men running ahead or when otherwise absolutely necessary – which means if a guerrilla comes down the hill. Any questions before we start?'

'Yes,' Taff called out. 'What happens if one of us is wounded and can't move on?'

'He stays where he lies. We can't afford to go back for him.'

'Charming!' Ben exclaimed.

'The priority is for some of us to get out and, if necessary, bring back support to get the guerrillas off the ridge and rescue those left behind.'

'Nice one,' Taff said sceptically.

'We don't have a choice,' Jimbo said. 'We have to keep going. If you fall, you remain where you are and that's all there is to it. Any *more* questions?'

The silence signified that there were no further questions, so Dead-eye said: 'All right. We leave in strict file formation. First me and Jimbo. Then Ben and Taff. Then Larry. Les and Ken leave last. Everyone agree?'

Again, everyone except Ken called out that they agreed.

'So let's do it,' Dead-eye whispered to Jimbo.

Both of them raised themselves slightly from the crouch, preparing to make the first run. Glancing up at the ridge, they saw that the guerrillas had spread out right along it, for what looked like at least half a mile, and were pointing their rifles at the wadi basin.

Aware that they were about to run a potentially lethal gauntlet, Dead-eye and Jimbo glanced at one another, held their breath, nodded and burst out from behind their cover, bolting for the nearest large rock.

Instantly, a storm of gunfire shattered the silence and filled the wadi around the running men with ricocheting bullets and geysering sand and dust. As Dead-eye and Jimbo ran forward, crouched low, zigzagging, the men behind them fired their SLRs at the guerrillas up on the ridge, not expecting to hit many but hoping to keep as many as possible pinned down. Dead-eye and Jimbo practically hurled themselves the last few feet, falling belly down, supporting themselves on one hand, then rolling over into shelter as bullets thudded into the ground just behind them and zipped off the rock at all angles.

'Made it!' Jimbo said breathlessly.

When both of them had scrambled up into the kneeling position, Dead-eye saw that some of the guerrillas, frustrated at hitting no one, were making their way down the hill. Taking aim, he waited until Ben and Taff had started on their own run before squeezing the trigger on single shot. The two troopers were halfway across when one of the Arabs on the hill threw his arms up, dropped his weapon, flopped backwards, then tumbled noisily in a slide of stones and gravel down the steep, rocky hill. By the time he had crashed lifeless into a boulder, the pair had made it behind their own rock and were preparing to give covering fire to those behind them.

'Next!' Jimbo bawled.

Larry was up and running like a bolt of lightning, zigzagging through spitting sand and small explosions of dust until he could fling himself behind another rock. The moment he was safe, he prepared to give covering fire to Ken and Les. The latter tugged his mate to his feet, said something to him, firmly took hold of his elbow, then shouted: 'Run!' Surprisingly, Ken obeyed, crouched low and zigzagging, missed by whistling bullets and flying stones, until they were practically at their chosen refuge.

It was then that Ken's leg gave out and he fell to his knees, cursed loudly, jerked free of Les, and turned around to aim his SLR at the ridge and fire a short burst on automatic. Two guerrillas who had been darting nimbly down the hill were hurled back by the rapid burst, dropped their weapons, then rolled a good way until they, too, were stopped by boulders.

Les darted back, grabbed his dazed comrade by the arm, and jerked him down behind a rock just as the ground where he had been kneeling was turned into a storm of spewing sand and boiling dust.

'Christ!' Jimbo muttered.

They started again, first Dead-eye and Jimbo, then the others, the running men covered by the others until it was their turn. On the second run, Ken was completely in control, albeit tugged along by Les, but on the third he jerked free again to fire another burst up the hill, this time hitting no one, but again continuing to fire in a crazed frenzy until dragged on by his friend.

Miraculously, neither was hit, though Les, whose own leg was still inflamed, practically collapsed behind the rock, almost sobbing with pain.

'They won't make it,' Jimbo said to Dead-eye.

'Then we leave them,' Dead-eye said.

They jumped up and ran again, weaving through the hail of bullets and making it to the safety of another rock. The three behind them did the same, all reaching safety, but Ken's leg gave way again, causing him to fall and curse in frustration. As Les dropped to his knees beside him, giving him covering fire and yelling at him to get up and run, the ground just in front of them erupted in spitting sand and boiling dust from a fresh hail of .303 bullets.

Ken stood up in full view, aimed his SLR at the guerrillas trying to drop down to the lower slopes, and fired a lengthy burst at those nearest him. Once more, he hit a couple, who fell, tumbling down the slope like rag dolls.

A bullet smashed into Ken's shoulder, making him spin to the side, drop his rifle and fall to his knees, crying out with the pain of this fresh wound. Les also dived sideways as a line of spitting sand snaked towards him, then between him and Ken. The latter hurled himself towards Les and they crashed together in a cloud of boiling sand behind another rock.

Breaking Dead-eye's ruling that no one should turn back, Larry backtracked, dodging lines of spitting sand and ricocheting bullets, until he was with Les and Ken. While the others waited for him, he roughly dressed Ken's bloody shoulder, at least stopping the flow of blood. He then jumped up and dashed back to his original position, narrowly escaping death a second time.

When Dead-eye and Jimbo jumped up and ran forward it all started again.

So they made their way along the wadi, alternately running erratically through a murderous hail of bullets and providing covering fire for the others.

Surprisingly, the wound in Ken's right shoulder, which prevented him from firing his SLR, seemed to have startled him back to some semblance of awareness and now he was no longer stopping during the dangerous runs. As his weapon had, anyway, been left behind in the wadi where he was wounded, he was able to use his arms for better balance when he made the dangerous runs on his wounded leg, hopping along in an ungainly manner.

As for the others, miraculously no one was hurt, and two hours later – the time it took to travel less than two miles – they were approaching the end of the wadi.

The guerrillas, who had followed them all the way, were now perched on the western end of the ridge, parallel to where the wadi opened out into flat, featureless desert. This was where the SAS men would make their escape and it was, ironically, where they would be most exposed.

Safely sheltered behind a group of large boulders at the very end of the wadi, Dead-eye looked up at the Arabs massed on the ridge, then across the featureless desert plain that ran for less than a mile to the Dhala Road and, not too far along it, the Thumier base.

'It's only a quarter of a mile,' Jimbo said hopefully.

'We'll never make it,' Dead-eye said.

They were silent for a long time, both deep in thought, until eventually Jimbo looked up and said: 'We can't stay here for ever.'

'I know,' Dead-eye replied. He glanced up to the ridge and saw that an increasing number of guerrillas were making their way down to the lower slopes, having surmised that the SAS were running out of ammunition and would, if they were forced to fight back, run out completely.

'Smart bastards,' Dead-eye said. 'And absolutely dedicated. They're willing to die charging us to make us run out of ammunition. When we do, the survivors will just march down and cut us to pieces. You've got to admire them.'

'I do,' Jimbo replied. 'I'm forming a fan club

for them. In the meantime, while I print up the letterhead, how do we keep my heroes at bay and still save our ammo?'

'We can't,' Dead-eye confessed.

'So?'

'I say we take a gamble. We gamble that if we start a fire-fight, the sentries at Thumier will hear us and come to the rescue.'

'The gamble being whether the cavalry get here before we run out of ammo or after we've been overrun.'

'I knew you'd understand, Jimbo.'

An urgent Chinese parliament produced agreement from the rest of the men, including Ken, who, though twice wounded and clearly on the brink of collapse, had at least regained his presence of mind.

'We better start soon,' he said, pointing up at the ridge. 'They're coming down to get us.'

Glancing up, they saw that the Arab guerrillas were indeed starting to swarm down the hill like ants, making their way from one rock to another with the skill of mountain goats. Some of them were already halfway down. They all had curved swords on their hips, supplementing their rifles.

'Spread out among these rocks,' said Dead-eye.

'Fix bayonets. Start firing at my signal. We have to make the fire-fight last as long as possible, so only fire on single shot. Any questions?'

'Yes,' Ken said from where he was leaning against a rock, one arm in a sling, his bloody wounded leg stretched out before him, 'what about me?'

'What about you?'

'I don't have an SLR.'

'Then you wait until they get within range and use your 9-milli to pick them off.' Dead-eye unholstered his own Browning, then gave it and his ammunition to Ken. 'Take this as a spare. Try not to use it until they get really close. You can protect yourself, and give us backup if we get involved in a CQB situation. That's it, men, let's shake out.'

The instant they broke apart and ran at the crouch to their respective rocks, the guerrillas on the hills let rip with a hail of rifle fire. The SAS men all managed to find shelter just as the enemy bullets tore up the sand between them and bounced noisily off the rocks, spraying them with flying fragments. As soon as he saw that his men were ready, Dead-eye gave the signal to fire.

'Fire at will!' he bawled, raising and lowering his right fist.

The SLRs roared in unison, picking off the Arabs who were now scrambling down the lower half of the slope. Instantly, the area being covered by the guerrillas turned into a maelstrom of spitting sand, swirling dust and shattered rock as the SLRs' bullets tore the ground up and wounded or dead Arabs rolled down the hill, their jellabas flapping wildly about them. Immediately, the guerrillas higher up the ridge unleashed another fusillade on the SAS positions, turning them into a similar hell of sand, dust and rebounding bullets.

Kneeling beside his friend, Les narrowly missed losing an eye when a bullet blew chunks off the rock and a sharp stone slashed across his left cheekbone. Temporarily blinded by his own blood, he cursed, checked the wound with his fingers and realized that the skin was hanging loose. Seeing Les's predicament, and not yet in a position to take part in the fire-fight, Ken removed a surgical dressing from his belt, and with trembling hands pressed the flapping, bloody skin back into position and applied the dressing. Meanwhile the other men around them kept firing at the advancing guerrillas. When Ken had finished dressing the wound and crawled back to cover, Les gamely picked up his SLR and began firing again.

The clouds of sand and dust created on the lower slopes by the combination of bullets and rolling bodies formed a screen that partially obscured the other guerrillas and allowed many of them to slip down unscathed. The first of them were now bursting through the suspended sand and dust and racing across the bed of the wadi, some firing from the hip, others swinging their curved swords above their heads. Most of them were cut down in a hail of SAS bullets, but the rest kept coming and those cut down were followed by others.

Lying belly down behind his rock, in great pain but more aware of feeling useless and frustrated, Ken smiled when he saw the guerrillas advancing. 'That's it,' he whispered, unholstering his Browning and lying it on the ground by his wounded leg. 'Keep coming, you bastards.' Still holding Dead-eye's 9-milli in his good hand, he released the safety-catch, rested his wrist on the rock, and took aim. 'Just keep coming,' he whispered.

Dead-eye had deliberately taken shelter behind a rock situated well in front of the others, from where he was methodically, unerringly picking off one guerrilla after another, particularly those racing up on either flank. But now, as the surviving Arabs raced straight across the wadi towards him, he saw that those massed on the summit of the ridge had begun to swarm down it as well, eager to hasten the massacre of the SAS troops. Realizing that time was running out and that he would soon be engaged in hand-to-hand fighting, he switched to automatic and started firing in a series of short, savage, lethal bursts that made the advancing guerrillas shudder, jerk, twist sideways and finally collapse amid clouds of exploding sand and billowing dust.

'Grenade!' Jimbo bawled.

Dead-eye saw the hand-grenade sail languidly over his head and fall behind him. He glanced back over his shoulder as it exploded near Ben and Taff, picking up the latter in a fountain of spewing soil and boiling smoke, spinning him over and slamming him back down a few feet away. Without thinking, Ben scrambled out from behind the rock, firing his SLR on the move, to kneel beside the dazed Taff, grab him by the shoulder and shake him back to awareness even as rebel bullets stitched the ground on all sides of them. 'Christ, Taff, get up! Move it!' With his face and body grazed by shrapnel and blistered by the blast,

Taff was not a pretty sight. Nevertheless, he sat up, shook his head from side to side, saw the lines of spitting sand moving in on all sides and, suddenly galvanized back to his senses, grabbed his SLR and scrambled back behind the rock with his friend. They both recommenced firing immediately.

As the lead guerrillas raced up to Dead-eye's position, where he was rising to his feet and firing from the hip, Jimbo, right behind him, realized that the need to save ammunition was past, and switched to automatic as well. The nearest Arab was swinging his sword at Dead-eye's head when Jimbo fired his first short burst, catching the enemy across the stomach, practically cutting him in two, and making him collapse like a blood-soaked banner. Dead-eye, meanwhile, had fired his last shots and was thrusting upwards at another guerrilla with his bayonet. Jimbo therefore made it his business to give Dead-eye cover, cutting down the Arabs nearest to him while Dead-eye expertly stabbed one, cracked the skull of another with the plastic stock, ducked to avoid a second swinging sword and, before coming up, stabbed his bayonet through the man's foot, pinning him to the ground and making him scream terribly, before removing the bayonet and plunging it through his heart.

Even before the Arab had fallen, Dead-eye had heaved the bloody bayonet out again and was turning to face another assault, moving coolly and murderously.

While Dead-eye was thus engaged, other Arabs rushed around him on both sides and came straight at Jimbo, who fired the last of his ammunition, then prepared to defend himself with his bayonet.

Meanwhile Ken was helping the lethal pair by carefully picking off any Arabs coming up on one of their blind sides. Lying belly down on the ground, his bloody, wounded leg stretched out behind him, he was propping himself up on his wounded arm and methodically firing one shot after another from Dead-eye's Browning. When he had emptied this, he picked up his own and began the same methodical procedure with it. Each time he fired, an agonizing pain shot through his wounded shoulder, yet it failed to stop him. He saved Dead-eye and Jimbo from death many times, though neither was aware of it.

Suddenly, the combined roaring of 76mm QF and .30-inch machine-guns resounded over the general din of the battle. Almost simultaneously, a murderous rain of bullets tore through the guerrillas behind those already at the SAS positions and made the area all around them explode in a convulsion of sand, soil, dust and pulverized rock. As the guerrillas to the immediate front were screaming and dying, a hail of bullets from another set of 76mm QF and .30-inch machine-guns started inflicting the same fate on the guerrillas swarming down from the summit of the ridge, cutting bloody swathes through them and making most of them retreat back the way they had come.

Glancing left at the same time, Dead-eye and Jimbo, both still engaged in furious hand-to-hand fighting, saw two 6×6 Saladins, machine-guns blazing, trundling across the plain from the direction of the Dhala Road. While the two armoured cars were heading straight for the besieged SAS troop, another two had broken away towards the lower slopes of the ridge, cutting off the line of retreat of the guerrillas engaged with the SAS and concentrating their fire on the Arabs now attempting to escape back up the ridge. The guerrillas not slaughtered in the vicious inferno of machine-gun fire were heading back the way they had come, along the summit of the ridge, in frantic disorder.

Exhilarated, Jimbo turned back to the fray just as the Arabs in front of Dead-eye were either being cut down by the Saladins or trying to make their escape across the wadi. Behind him, however, Larry had just fired his final bullets at two guerrillas, killing one and making the other turn around and flee. Swinging his sword automatically at Jimbo as he passed, the Arab caught his arm, opening it from shoulder to elbow and exposing the bone beneath the skin.

Screaming, Jimbo dropped his SLR, slapped his left hand over his arm where the blood was pouring out of it, and fell to his knees. The guerrilla, rushing away, was shot in the back of the head with the last bullet from Ben's SLR and lunged forward, his arms flung above his bloody, smashed skull, to fall face first to the ground – as did Jimbo, from shock and loss of blood.

The few guerrillas still remaining at the SAS positions now turned and fled back towards the wadi, but found their retreat blocked by the two Saladins crossing the lower slopes to fire at the guerrillas retreating along the top of the ridge. The other two Saladins kept raining fire on the guerrillas in the wadi, even when they had reached the SAS positions. There, while the two gunners continued firing, the third crew member climbed down to hand out more SLR ammunition to the SAS men still standing.

Dead-eye, Larry, Ben and the bloody, blistered Taff therefore had the pleasure of helping to rout the last of the fleeing guerrillas. Even Ken had crawled through the sand to pick up the unconscious Jimbo's SLR, load it with ammo given to him by the British Army corporal, and make amends for his moments of shock-induced madness by expertly dispatching the last two fleeing guerrillas, firing from the belly-down position, using one arm. He passed out within seconds of having done so.

When the other two Saladins had chased the surviving guerrillas far enough along the wadi to know that they would not come back, they radioed the Habilayn airstrip, asking for air support to clear the last of the guerrillas off the summit of the ridge. They were returning to help the other two Saladins pick up the SAS men when two Hawker Hunters roared low over the ridge and poured a devastating hail of gunfire into the fleeing guerrillas. By the time the two Saladins had reached the SAS men, the summit of the ridge was obscured by an immense cloud of dust and smoke which mercifully concealed the many dead below.

The few survivors crawled out of that pall of smoke and limped back to the Radfan.

While the Hawker Hunters flew back to Habilayn, the four Saladins shared the SAS troop between them. Jimbo's badly sliced right arm was given interim treatment by Larry, who closed it with emergency sutures and stopped the bleeding with a tourniquet and bandages; then the still unconscious sergeant was hoisted up into one of the Saladins.

He was followed in by Les and Larry, the latter intending to replace the blood-soaked emergency bandage on Les's cheek as the Saladin carried them back to the base.

In the second Saladin, Ben and Taff were not in much better shape. The lengthy, scorched gouge across Riley's back had been reopened during the hand-to-hand fighting and was now bleeding profusely, soaking through his tattered shirt and dripping on the steel floor. As for Taff, though the scars of his shrapnel-shredded face would heal eventually, right now, in combination with the blisters caused by the heat of the grenade explosion, they made for a stomach-churning sight.

With his wounded shoulder and twice-wounded left leg, Ken had to be helped into the third

Saladin by the third crew member, Corporal Phil Rossiter. Ken had regained consciousness and was surprisingly alert. After making him comfortable, the Regular Army man turned to Dead-eye, still standing beside the Saladin, and said: 'You men did a hell of a job out there, Sarge. You should be proud of yourselves.'

'We did nothing,' Dead-eye said to Rossiter with icy rage. 'The Saladins did the job. The Hawker Hunters did the job. *You* did it. We didn't do a damned thing! This war stinks to high heaven.' Then, having vented his spleen, he stomped off angrily to take his place in the fourth armoured car.

Corporal Rossiter turned in amazement to Ken. 'What the hell's the matter with him?' he asked. 'Is it because you lost two of your men?'

'Not because we lost them,' Ken replied. 'It's because the Arabs captured the bodies. That's what's eating Dead-eye . . . It could have repercussions.'

'It surely could,' Corporal Rossiter replied dryly, before climbing into the Saladin.

Growling aggressively, the four armoured cars trundled away from the wadi, back across the flat, dusty desert plain, to the tarmacked Dhala Road and, farther along it, the SAS base at Thumier, leaving a pile of dead bodies in the sand as food for the vultures.

It was that kind of war.

17

The operation begun by the SAS in the mountains of the Radfan was continued by the Paras and 45 Royal Marine Commando, who climbed and fought their way up the 3700-foot Al Hajaf hills, where most of the guerrillas were based. The same operation was completed by six major units which, between them, managed to subdue the area five weeks later. The inhabitants were then banished from the region.

A few days after the SAS had returned to Thumier, a macabre intelligence report regarding the fate of the bodies of Captain Ellsworth and Trooper Malkin reached Major-General John Gibbon, the General Officer Commanding in Aden. According to a Radio Taiz Yemeni propaganda broadcast, the heads of the two dead soldiers had been put on public display in the Yemen.

Asked to verify this at a press conference held on 3 May 1964, the GOC confirmed that he had received 'reliable information of their decapitation and the exhibition of their heads on stakes in Yemen'.

This response was to lead to singular embarrassment for the security forces, as the next of kin had been unaware of the deaths and, even worse, had been informed that the men were on a routine exercise on Salisbury Plain.

Following hot on the heels of Major-General Gibbon's press conference, the republican government in Yemen, denying its own propaganda broadcast, denounced the decapitation story as a 'British lie'.

In Taiz, the US Embassy, which was handling British interests in the absence of UK diplomatic recognition of the republicans, investigated the matter and concluded that there was no truth in the rumours that the heads of two British soldiers had been exhibited in the Yemen or anywhere else.

However, ten days after the press conference, confirmation was received that a patrol of the Federal Regular Army had found two headless bodies buried in a shallow grave in the area of the SAS battle. There was no sign of the heads.

For a brief period after their return to Britain, D Squadron SAS became the subject of intense interest to the press. But once this had faded and the squadron had returned to its former anonymity, it went back to serving periodically in Aden during retraining periods between each stint in the jungles of Borneo.

Dead-eye, Jimbo and the other survivors of the first campaign were back in the Radfan when the British withdrew in 1967. Once again, they divided their time between desert and mountain and the lethal Keeni-Meeni actions in Aden. No longer interested in this pointless war, the SAS men in the mountains tried to kill their boredom by endlessly speculating on the good time their mates, the 'urbanites', were having in the flesh-pots of Aden. When in the city, the same men vented their frustration by complaining about the overcrowded *souks*, the treachery of the Arabs and the ineptitude of the 'greens' guarding the streets.

'They stand there at each street corner like limp dicks at a wedding,' Jimbo complained. 'The Arabs should be blowing them kisses, not trying to kill 'em. The British Army! God help us!'

'What we're doing is just as worthless,' Dead-eye

replied in his quiet, bitter way. 'We're just passing time.'

Nevertheless, the nearer the projected withdrawal date came, the more essential were the SAS recce patrols, to give early warning of guerrilla attacks. The guerrillas, in turn, were now receiving early warnings of SAS movements from Arab officers of the FRA who knew that when the British left, their own lives would depend on how helpful they had been to the rebel forces.

The Radfan was handed over to the Federal Regular Army – now the South Arabian Army – on 26 June 1967, at the end of the Six Day War between Israel and Egypt, which led to the singular humiliation of Arab Nationalists and riots in the streets of many Muslim cities.

'This fight's long been a dying cause,' a disillusioned Lieutenant-Colonel Callaghan told his men just before they boarded the Hercules C-130 on the runway at RAF Khormaksar. 'Now, at last, it's been lost.'

No one disagreed as the heavy transport plane lifted off the ground, ascending through the shimmering heat, to deliver them back to RAF Lyneham. From there they would be transported in a convoy of Bedfords to their camp at Bradbury Lines,

Hereford, where, on their bashas, in the chilly darkness of the spider, they would finally rest, trying to forget the nightmares of the Radfan and looking forward to better days.

'Bloody right!' Jimbo exclaimed as the Hercules climbed into the radiant sky. 'Better days always come.'

'There speaks the optimist,' Dead-eye replied, then smiled sadly before closing his weary eyes.

It would be a long flight.